"We all aspire to do great things, but sometimes we lack the passion to make them happen. *The Dream-Centered Life* gives us a blueprint to help us discover our motives and overcome barriers that can derail our dreams. I encourage you to read this book and find your dream."

—JOHN C. MAXWELL, author, speaker, and founder
of the John Maxwell Company

"Discouragement can peek around every corner and extinguish passions and dreams. Bask in the refreshing light of encouragement from Luke Barnett as he navigates the amazing plans God has for every dreamer."

—ROMA DOWNEY, actress, producer, and president
of LightWorkers Media

"In *The Dream-Centered Life*, Luke Barnett reveals the secret to making your dreams come true: drawing closer to God and depending on him each step of the way. Luke inspires us to take our God-given dreams seriously and then shows us how to bring them to life with God's help."

—CHRIS HODGES, senior pastor of Church of the Highlands
and author of *Fresh Air*

"*The Dream-Centered Life* is a must-read for anyone who wants to see their calling fulfilled. Luke Barnett challenges you to stand up, wipe off the dirt, and climb out of the predictable to find your dream."

—JOHN BEVERE, author and minister at Messenger International

"Luke Barnett believes we can create our future and it starts with a dream. He then inspires us to dream bigger. His practical and spiritual way empowers us to believe we can dream and see it come to pass. If you want to see great things, read *The Dream-Centered Life*."

—CASEY TREAT, senior pastor of Christian Faith Center
and coauthor of *Renewing the Mind 2.0*

"Dreams are the substance of all great achievement. I'm thrilled that my friend Luke Barnett has written such a practical book on the importance of dreaming and the process through which our dreams become reality. Luke has lived what is taught within these pages!"

—Bishop Dale C. Bronner, DMin, senior pastor of Word of Faith Family Worship Cathedral

"Everything of value starts with a dream—a God-given vision of our greater purpose. This book will teach you how to dream again and how to take the steps needed to make those dreams a reality."

—Todd Mullins, senior pastor of Christ Fellowship Church

"The only dream that is fulfilling and worth pursuing is a God-given dream. Luke Barnett lives out his God-given dream daily, and in this book he clearly explains how you, too, can get your dream back."

—Rick Bezet, lead pastor of New Life Church of Arkansas and author of *Real Love in an Angry World*

"This book challenges readers to live a life with purpose. Luke lays out simple steps we all can take to allow God to restore our dreams."

—Jentezen Franklin, senior pastor of Free Chapel and *New York Times* best-selling author

"My brother, Luke Barnett, is a perfect example of how to dream big! *The Dream-Centered Life* offers great examples and instruction on how to believe for big, God-based dreams for your life."

—Matthew Barnett, cofounder of the Dream Center and *New York Times* best-selling author of *The Cause Within You*

"God-given dreams are possible and should be sought wholeheartedly. Life's challenges can derail our aspirations. Luke Barnett helps readers get back on track to living out God's amazing plan for their lives."

—Mark Batterson, *New York Times* best-selling author of *The Circle Maker* and lead pastor of National Community Church

THE DREAM CENTERED LIFE

DISCOVERING WHAT DRIVES YOU

LUKE BARNETT

WATERBROOK

THE DREAM-CENTERED LIFE

Trade Paperback ISBN 978-0-7352-8965-9
eBook ISBN 978-0-7352-8966-6

Cover design by Mark D. Ford

Published in the United States by WaterBrook, an imprint of the Crown Publishing Group, a division of Penguin Random House LLC, New York.

WATERBROOK® and its deer colophon are registered trademarks of Penguin Random House LLC.

Library of Congress Cataloging-in-Publication Data
Names: Barnett, Luke, author.
Title: The dream-centered life / Luke Barnett.
Description: First Edition. | Colorado Springs, Colorado : WaterBrook, 2017.
Identifiers: LCCN 2017013308 | ISBN 9780735289659 (pbk.) | ISBN 9780735289666 (electronic)
Subjects: LCSH: Dreams—Religious aspects—Christianity. | Joseph (Son of Jacob)
Classification: LCC BR115.D74 B35 2017 | DDC 248.2/9—dc23
LC record available at https://lccn.loc.gov/2017013308

Printed in the United States of America
2017—First Edition

10 9 8 7 6 5 4 3 2 1

SPECIAL SALES
Most WaterBrook books are available at special quantity discounts when purchased in bulk by corporations, organizations, and special-interest groups. Custom imprinting or excerpting can also be done to fit special needs. For information, please e-mail specialmarketscms@penguin randomhouse.com or call 1-800-603-7051.

To my family

My wife, Angel, you have stuck with me from the beginning of this journey and kept an incredible inspirational attitude through the ups and downs. You have been a tremendous source of life and encouragement to me for the last twenty-three years.

My daughters, Aubrey and Annalee, you are so full of life and bring such joy to your mother and me. Annalee, I love your inner drive and persistence. When you set your mind to do something, you do it! Aubrey, I love your creativity and how you bring life and energy to a party just by walking into the room.

Mom, you're an overcomer and a fighter. You taught me to never give up and to always keep looking forward to the future.

Dad, you're the one who taught me that anything is possible when you partner with God in dreaming. I've watched you live your life to its fullest, enjoying every single moment of each day. Your love for life, especially in your later years, has motivated me to want to pattern my life after you and someday be the man you are.

Contents

Introduction

When I was a kid, if you had told me I would one day stand on the platform of my dad's church in Phoenix, accept the baton representing his ministry, and take leadership of the church I had grown up in, I would have laughed until it was clear how ridiculous your suggestion was. There was no way I was going to be a pastor. A golfer, maybe, if I could continue to improve. Or maybe a businessman, a consultant, or a CEO. But a pastor? In the church my dad built? No way.

Yet there I was in front of thousands accepting essentially my life commission. My mom was there, and Dad, of course. My wife, Angel, stood right beside me. This was as close to a formal ceremony as you were likely to see in our church. Part of me was in awe that God had brought me to a place of actually wanting to follow my father in ministry. Another part of me wondered if I would wake up and realize I was having a kind of tailor-made nightmare.

More than anything, I felt the profound weight of leading the thousands of people who called Phoenix First Assembly their church family. I gripped Angel's hand and with the other I held the golden-colored baton that had been given to my dad by Dr. Bill Bright, one of the great Christian leaders of modern times. It represented five million people trained in ministry, an almost unfathomable number for one man to influence, as my dad had done.

Tommy Barnett, my father, is one of the great innovators and visionaries who led the twentieth-century church. History books will record what he did, but more important to my dad is how he inspired so many people to believe they could achieve their God-given destinies and dreams. Really, there's no one else on the planet like Tommy Barnett. I knew that even growing up. The effect he has on people is nothing short of supernatural. Just being around him, people believe in themselves and what they can accomplish. So many ministries were birthed in his churches because he simply believed in and loved people.

If I hadn't grown up in his household, I probably would have been more intimidated by my dad's example. For some reason I was always confident enough to believe that he had his gifts and I had mine, though they seemed very different. When people praised my dad, I went along with it and agreed or sometimes rolled my eyes if they got too effusive. Maybe it's because he made ministry look easy, like when you're ten years old and watch your parent drive and think, *I could do that. Just put me behind the wheel.*

At that moment as I held the baton, I was behind the wheel, and the road ahead looked a lot different than it did when Dad was driving. As I received that baton of ministry and prepared to steer the congregation Dad had built, I felt something new: an almost crushing weight of expectation. The service ended, I shook hundreds of hands, and when I woke up the next morning, it was as if someone had flipped a switch on my emotions. I fell into what I can best describe as a sudden depression. I was forty-three years old, had been in ministry twenty years, and now feared I didn't have what it would take to lead where God had placed me. I was a man without a dream, a leader without a vision. A little voice told me over and over, "You're dead in the water. You'll never live up to this legacy. You don't have what it takes to lead this organization."

My personal inventory of talents suddenly seemed small. I had some natural teaching and administrative gifts and was good at relating to people personally. Those strengths had served me well in smaller settings. But I had never come close to leading a world-class ministry like this one, built by one of the great visionaries of our day. So I did what every good leader does at some point: I began to panic.

Over the next few months, God taught me more about leadership—and life—than I had learned in the previous twenty years. In my desperation, I suddenly saw exactly what I needed—and what every person needs: *a God-given dream.*

Everything of any value starts with a dream.

Everything.

Every business, every relationship, every invention, every story, every journey, every worthwhile day of our lives begins with a dream. By *dream* I mean a revelation of what we should be doing, a vision of our greater purpose. Having a dream is the difference between life and death, thriving or existing, leading or faking it.

To be honest, I didn't realize I had been moving through life without a dream. It's easy to convince ourselves that we're doing everything correctly, living at the highest level possible, achieving and enjoying all life has to offer. But I'm here to tell you there is another level that you may not have experienced yet. I didn't experience it until I was in my forties. It surprised me when I discovered it. It also radically changed my life and allowed me to succeed in the almost overwhelming task I have been given. Before hitting that crisis and discovering the dream, I wasn't one-tenth of the leader I came to be in the next short years.

Each of us comes to critical moments when same ol' same ol' won't cut it. When the regular routine becomes reckless. When we realize we are lacking a key for the door in front of us. That missing key is a dream. Finding God's dream for you can make life worth living.

In the pages that follow, I will help you find your dream, one that will carry you the rest of your life and make you want to get up in the morning and slay every dragon. We will talk about how to make a radical break from the norm, if necessary, to catch the new vision. We will talk about the habits and thought patterns of a dreamer, which I have learned from living around dreamers all my life and much later becoming one myself. In very practical ways, I will discuss what it takes to dream effectively, no matter your starting point.

These principles work universally. You don't have to be a pastor or minister; you don't even have to belong to a church or share my precise belief system. Like gravity and the laws of nature, the principles of dreaming work across the board. You can road test them. You can watch them work for you.

What I know is this: if I can go from being a moderately successful leader of smaller organizations to a vision-fueled, dream-centered leader of a world-class organization, you can grow in a similar way, whatever circumstance you're in. You may be a businessperson, a consultant, an entrepreneur, a blogger, a mom, a factory worker, a volunteer, a teacher, a scuba diver, or someone in an entirely different role. The invitation to a dream-centered life is for you.

It's time to dream.

PART ONE

Journey to a Dream

1

Dreamless in Disneyland

Everything starts with a dream, and if you don't have a dream of your own, you will live someone else's. I was doing just that as I clung to the cold metal fence that surrounds Disneyland, with friends I probably shouldn't have been hanging out with. My mom and dad's words rang in my mind: *"Luke, you're going to college. Please, don't hang around with fools."*

Oh, well. Blew that one, I thought as I hoisted myself up and over.

It was 2:00 a.m. How had they convinced me to sneak into the "Happiest Place on Earth" in the middle of the night? The idea had seemed crazy when someone first mentioned it, but after a few hours of psyching ourselves up, it felt almost normal. Now I was jumping over the fence and landing on the vegetation on the other side. I was officially in Disneyland. I expected alarms to go off or something—laser beams, bright spotlights, men with dogs. But there was nothing. No security alarms. No electric fencing or bright lights.

Maybe this won't be so bad after all, I thought. *We can walk around a little while, then come out the way we came in. No sweat.*

My buddies and I crept inward toward what appeared to be Frontierland. We hopped over the railroad tracks, carefully staying in the shadows. Strangely, the park was brightly lit by huge industrial lights, but nobody was there. Everything was awash in a kind of acid-white work light. No rides were running. There was no music. The silence and stillness were ghostly.

Speaking of ghosts, we walked first into the Haunted Mansion. It was no longer dim and spooky. Instead it looked like a hotel lobby at night, even somewhat inviting.

"Hey, let's see what Pirates looks like," said a friend. We all followed him toward the Pirates of the Caribbean ride. Sure enough, the inside was all lit up and empty. Gone was the night sky, the dancing fireflies, the southern ambience, the music and rushing water. It was simply a big room, still impressive, but no longer mysterious. I could hardly believe it was the same place.

"This is crazy. There's nobody here," a friend said, and as we exited the way we came in, we felt bolder. Instead of hiding in the shadows we walked down the middle of the street toward Adventureland.

That's when a security guard appeared, riding over the hill on his bicycle. "Guys! What are you doing! Stop!" he yelled.

We screamed, panicked, and scattered. I found myself sprinting toward the Jungle Cruise. There I found a place to hide among the plants. A tiger was staring me in the face, and hippos were coming up out of the river. I could smell the dirt and bleach from the water.

I hope they don't use security dogs, I thought. *I'm a sitting duck.*

Within moments, dozens of security people were scouring the park for us. I could see their flashlights and hear their voices. Gone was my sense of excitement and bravery. Now I felt desperate. I fashioned one escape plan after another in my mind as I listened and heard the guards apprehending my buddies. After a while it just didn't seem worth it anymore. These guys knew the park and knew how to do their jobs. They were going to find me. I preferred to surrender myself peacefully than be caught on the run. Also, my conscience was working on me and I wanted relief. I stepped out of my hiding place and into the street. Guards came over and took hold of me. We began walking . . . somewhere.

I was just eighteen. I wasn't a bad kid, just young and naive and not really committed to anything. I had come as a freshman to a Christian college in Southern California to play baseball. For a short season I fell into some bad habits and less-than-awesome friendships. Whatever notion I had that my Christian upbringing would rub off on these guys proved the opposite: they rubbed off on me a lot more. I was finding that sin was fun for a while but in the end it always exacted a higher price than I wanted to pay.

Now my friends and I got to see the inside of the security building at Disneyland. It didn't look nearly as fun as the rest of the place. Nobody felt like putting on mouse ears, that's for sure. A police officer soon arrived. She asked us a bunch of questions. Why did we sneak in? What were we trying to do? Was there anyone else in our group? Where had we entered the park?

Finally, she said, "I'm going to write you a citation for trespassing. Don't you ever come back to Disneyland again. Now show me your ID."

I reached in my pocket. Nothing. I tried another pocket. Zilch. I had failed to bring any identification.

"I don't have any on me," I said, gulping my fear down and hoping this was not a major problem.

"That's bad news," she said. "I'm going to have to take you downtown for the night."

With that she slapped handcuffs on me and walked me to her police car. I got in the back.

I've been out of my dad's house for a few weeks, and here I am heading to a jail cell in Anaheim, I thought. *I don't even shave yet.* My heart stayed down near my shoes for the entire ride. *What am I doing? What are Dad and Mom going to think?*

When we arrived at the jail, the officer walked me through the women's cellblock first. There were all the prostitutes who had been arrested that night. I had long blond hair and looked about twelve years old because I was such a late bloomer. I weighed 112 pounds and stood five foot five.

"Whoo, baby!" they whooped and jeered at me. I kept my head down and watched my feet carry me across the floor.

"Bring him over here!" some taunted. Others whistled at me as I passed between their cells. They were getting a good laugh out of seeing a kid hauled in.

The officer ushered me to a cell where three men stood around talking: a very large white guy who looked like he'd been dragged out of a dumpster; a stocky African American guy, and a Native American guy. They were in a huddle talking about why they were there. The door clanged behind me.

"Barroom fight," I heard one guy say.

"Domestic violence," said another. Then they turned to me and seemed not to believe their eyes.

"Why are *you* here?" they asked, probably wondering why I wasn't in the juvenile ward.

I wanted to say, "I'm a serial killer," but I told the truth.

"I snuck into Disneyland. They caught me in the Jungle Cruise," I said.

That mystified them more than impressed them. Thankfully, they left me alone. I sat there awake the rest of the night, wondering why I hadn't been carrying any ID, why I had let myself be persuaded to do something so dumb as to trespass. Finally, as day broke, an officer retrieved me from the cell and took me into a court hearing where the judge looked at me and said, "Sneaking into Disneyland wasn't as fun as you thought it would be, was it? Time served." The gavel came down.

Some friends of mine were in the courtroom and drove me back to the college campus. When I arrived, the dean of the college called me into his office, and we had a very serious conversation about why I had come to that college and how I should conduct myself as a student. For reasons I still don't understand, the college didn't punish me and didn't even tell my parents. Life went on as usual.

IN NEED OF A PLAN

But the experience summarized my life in some way. At that point I was directionless and had no real identity, so I was defined by those around me. Like so many in this world, I was wandering around without knowing who I really was, where I was going, or what my dream in life was.

I moved home after that school year to try a different path. In high school I had done well athletically. I'd been selected for the all-conference team in baseball and had helped our golf team win the state championship. But I hadn't been able to compete well at the college level. It was time to seek a new direction.

One evening at dinner back in Phoenix, Dad randomly said, "Luke, I heard about what happened to you over in college."

I blushed to my collar.

"You did?" I said. "How come you never said anything?"

"I hear things," he said.

That's amazing, I thought. *I thought I hid it so well.*

"If you already know, then let me tell you how it really went down," I said and told the whole Disneyland story in detail. My mom and dad and brother, Matthew, listened with great interest, and when I finished, Dad shook his head and laughed for a long time.

"Luke, I had no idea about any of this," he said. "I just said that to see what you would say. You spilled all the beans right there."

I blushed again. I could never snooker my dad.

I think Dad could see how frustrated I was with trying to find my life purpose, because one day he sat me down and said, "Luke, what do you feel energized about doing?"

"I love to play golf," I said. "I'm pretty good and would love to play on the PGA tour one day."

"I think you ought to pursue that," he said. "I'll support you and pay for it. Just in case that doesn't pan out, I'm going to send you to Arizona State University and you're going to get a business administration degree too."

"It's a deal," I said.

I had already told him that I didn't feel called to ministry, and Dad discouraged his kids from going into ministry unless we really felt like we wanted to. He knew we couldn't sustain it if the desire didn't spring from our own hearts.

With a new plan in place, life improved for me. I attended ASU, played a lot of golf, and earned my local professional tour card.

In addition, Dad began taking me all over the world on his ministry trips, and I got to see great sights.

During that time some wealthy Christian businessmen arranged to bring leaders to different world-class resorts for special meetings. Some of these resorts were incredible, sought-after golf destinations such as Pinehurst in North Carolina, Pebble Beach in California, the Broadmoor in Colorado, and Kapalua on the island of Maui. My dad couldn't go because he was building the Los Angeles Dream Center (more about that later) and traveling almost every week. But he asked me, "They're footing the bill. Would you like to go and represent our church?"

Of course my answer was yes. I was in my twenties and traveling to amazing resorts, enjoying the finest things life had to offer. But I began to notice a common theme as I traveled from one to another. Couples in their sixties and seventies would walk around holding hands and saying things like, "Here we are, honey. We finally made it. Forty years of saving and working, and we finally arrived."

I thought to myself, *These people have worked their entire lives to arrive at this place, and I'm here at age twenty. If this is the best life has to offer—if this is "it" and I'm already experiencing it—I'm in big trouble.*

I was surrounded by luxury, but I began to feel I was dying on the inside. All my friends thought I had it made, but the truth is this season got old really quick. I sensed a slow wasting away in myself. All those perks lost their punch. One day I put my finger on why: I wasn't living out God's script for my life. I was just living out a script that Dad and I had written one day. Even though I technically had a set of plans and goals, I felt a sinking, perishing feeling.

I don't think I can stay fired up about my plans for the next forty or fifty years, I thought. *What am I going to do with the rest of my life?*

A FIRSTHAND REVELATION

I needed a revelation from God. So I did the only thing I knew to do: I got serious with God about it. I began seeking him. I even fasted for the first time in my adult life. I tried tuning my senses to hear God. I woke up every morning, went out by myself with a Bible and a notebook, and for hours just prayed, *Would you speak to me about my future?*

By this time I knew I wasn't going to be a professional golfer, though I would have liked to be one. I wasn't doing well enough on the mini tours in Arizona. Without golf and athletics, I didn't know who I was.

One day back home, Dad gave me a teaching series from Bill Hybels, the leader of a well-known church near Chicago. I began listening to it as I drove around, and for the first time felt excited about ministry work.

Though I was raised in a great church and a great home, I took both for granted a bit. Bill's perspective and his church's innovations excited me as I began to see what could be done in that arena.

Dad noticed I was paying attention to what Bill had to say, and he threw out a possibility: "If you ever get asked to speak in a church, just do it, Luke. Try it out. See if God would use you in that way."

It was a preposterous idea. I had never preached, I was young, and everyone around me knew I had no interest in church ministry. It was a safe promise to make.

"Sure," I said. "If someone calls me and asks me to preach, I will."

That'll never happen, I thought, and I put it out of my mind.

Two weeks later Eugene Heiskell, pastor of a small church in Goodyear, Arizona, called me out of the blue. I had never heard of the man.

"Luke," he said, "I don't even know you, but I feel very impressed to ask you to speak in my church on Sunday night."

"Did my dad put you up to this?" I blurted.

"No, I've never met your dad," he assured me.

"But I'm not a preacher," I said. "Why would you want me?"

"I just feel impressed to ask you," he said.

I got off the phone without committing and walked into Dad's office.

"You set me up," I said. "You put Eugene Heiskell up to this."

"What are you talking about?" Dad said. "I don't know who that is. Did he ask you to preach?"

"Yes," I said grudgingly.

"Well, you said if someone called, you would go."

I was stuck. I accepted the invitation, memorized one of Dad's sermons, and preached it to myself in the car as I drove out to Goodyear. It didn't even sound good coming back at me from the windshield. I had no idea how to preach. I felt certain I would go down in flames. *At least it's a small church,* I thought. *Fewer to witness the crime of the century as I murder this poor message.*

There were indeed just a couple dozen people there that night. As expected, I gave the worst sermon in the history of sermons. There was no flow to it, no sense of power, and my own enthusiasm ebbed as I felt myself failing and faltering through it. It was a train wreck, and I was the conductor. Everybody sat there watching it happen.

I can't wait to get home and go to bed, I thought.

I fumbled my way to the end and began to offer an invitation for people to meet Jesus. At that moment a strange shift happened. Suddenly I felt comfortable. My words came easily. There was a power there that hadn't been present the rest of the time. Somehow I knew what I was doing, what I should say, how to say it. I basked in the confidence of the moment and even lengthened it a bit.

One person stood up, an African American woman. She bravely walked down the aisle to signify her conversion to Christ, and in that moment things became crystal clear. I sensed God responding to all the prayers I had prayed in previous months. An assurance and excitement rose up in me that I could do this again and again without getting tired of it. Introducing people to Jesus seemed part of my life purpose.

As I drove home, I felt in a small way like Abraham in the Old Testament. He chose to take an unknown path based on faith, and that decision redirected his whole life.

The next week I walked into my dad's office.

"I'm done," I stated. "I'm giving up on the plan you and I came up with a few years ago. No more professional golf. No more pursuing a business degree at college. I have to follow the path I believe God has shown me."

Dad stood up, walked around his desk, and wrapped his arms around me. "Oh, Son," he said. "That's all I've ever wanted for your life—a firsthand revelation, and you've got it. I support you all the way. Go for it."

I never looked back. I still didn't know how to preach, how to lead people well, what to say. If I had known the battles that were right around the corner, I probably would have given up immediately. But one thing I knew: I felt alive, more than I did at those luxurious resorts or anywhere else. I had a purpose.

I was a long way from becoming a dreamer, but it was my first significant step as a leader.

POWER TO PREACH

Of course, I grew up in a type of leadership factory. Dad naturally inspired thousands of people to connect with their life callings, to see themselves as leaders and dreamers. Our church was like a leadership laboratory, and people came from all over the world to learn and be inspired.

Faiz Rahman, a professor at my dad's Bible school in Phoenix, had a dream to go back to India and start a Dream Center, a dynamic urban ministry first pioneered by my father and brother. Today thirty-one Dream Centers established by him provide food, clothing, medical care, and education to three thousand kids each month in India.

Sharon Henning is known to some as the Mother Teresa of Phoenix. She discovered her dream when Dad asked her to start a special-needs ministry at our church. At first, Sharon wasn't that interested. She didn't have a heart for special-needs people. But she prayed and asked God to expand her capacity to love. That led to twenty-six years of ministry to special-needs people in our community, with wheelchair buses helping to fill the front of our auditorium every week. Each summer

Sharon hosts a special-needs camp in Flagstaff with more than 150 people attending.

Those are inspiring stories, but when I decided to embark on a life of leadership, I was still in pretty rough shape. One night a bunch of us were playing basketball in our church gym as part of organized church activities. A kid showed up looking like a gangster. He was purposely knocking other kids into the bleachers when they went for layups. I got fed up and said, "Hey, pick on somebody your own size." From that point on, he went after me, fouling me and mocking me. The tension between us got so bad that the kids started to realize that the pastor's son was about to get into a fight with a neighborhood kid. The activities director wisely stopped the game.

"Everybody come over," she said. "Let's circle up and pray."

Twenty-five of us held hands and closed our eyes. I was trying to repent and get my heart right when I looked up and saw the guy standing across the circle from me blowing kisses at me in a mocking way. I got so furious I walked over right during the prayer and punched him in the face. I had never done anything like that before, but I have to say it felt good.

Of course, I had to apologize and make it right. That may have been one reason Dad suggested I go away for the summer to preach every week in small churches. I had a lot of maturing to do, and our family knew that the way to get better at preaching (or anything) is to do it over and over again.

When Dad's mom, Joy Barnett, heard about our plan, she said, "Why don't you send Luke to Kansas City? I'll set him up in churches here, and he can stay with me all summer and preach Sundays and Wednesdays."

I loved the idea. My grandparents had pastored for fifty-eight years in Kansas City and knew everybody there. My grandmother filled my preaching schedule, though I had preached only two times by then.

Dad's mom was a phenomenal woman—so very smart and encouraging. She always dressed well, and her skin looked like that of a thirty-year-old woman. She analyzed handwriting for the FBI and helped them track down criminals. She used that same skill as an icebreaker when counseling married couples. She could get them laughing by telling them things she could discern about them based on their handwriting. I called her a fortune-teller, but she was anything but. She was a motivator par excellence, always encouraging those around her to dream big. If anyone wonders where my dad got his visionary qualities, it was from her.

I stayed in the basement of her house—with its orange carpet and an assortment of wooden elephants and other gifts from missionaries who had stayed at the home. I knew only two sermons when I arrived and needed a few more if I was going to preach revivals Monday through Wednesday at some churches. I found it nerve racking trying to figure out what to say and spent most of my time in the basement studying for my next message. The aromas of breakfast and dinner would draw me upstairs where Grandmother made biscuits and gravy with country sausage for breakfast and, for dinner, tacos in homemade pan-fried corn tortillas with homemade apple pie for dessert.

Preaching at little churches of thirty and forty people gave me experience, but it also revealed one of my great weaknesses: I stuttered. As Grandmother drove me from church to church, I dreaded the thought of stuttering in front of the congregation. Some nights felt absolutely devastating.

One night while riding home with Grandmother, I broke down crying. I had struggled so much to get the message out that night.

"I just can't do this," I said in the midst of tears. "I'm not gifted. I'm slow of speech. I can't get my words out. I can't do it."

"Oh, you can do anything God calls you to, with his help," she said.

It was exactly what she always said, but this problem felt deeper, like something that could derail my entire ministry before it even began.

"I have an awful time getting through my messages," I continued. "My whole family can preach, but for me there's no flow or rhythm. I can't be called to do this. I'm not qualified for it."

For a few more minutes, I let the tears run down my face and voiced all my doubts. But as we approached the house, something rose up in me. I can't say it was my grandmother's encouragement, because it seemed to come from a different place. Suddenly I began to speak to myself, and my tears dried up: "That's not the right attitude," I said. "I don't care if it kills me. I'm going to study, work, pray, depend on God, and be God's messenger. I will lean on God and ask him to help me with this thorn in my flesh."

Grandmother looked at me deeply. She told me later that she knew she had witnessed a turning point in my life—the moment when I grabbed myself by the back of the neck and decided I wouldn't take no for an answer.

The stuttering problem didn't go away; in fact, I still struggle with it to this day. But I took great solace in Paul's description of the thorn in his flesh that God would not take away. For whatever reason, that thorn taught Paul about God's power and grace the way nothing else could. In the same way, even now I lean into God's grace every single time I stand before a church. I tell him, *God, I've studied and prayed, but without you I can't do it.* I know that deep down inside me is that stuttering problem, and it rises up from time to time. Every time I stand in that pulpit, I feel God saying, *My grace is sufficient for you, for my power is made perfect in your weakness.*

Having determined to lean on God and continue preaching, I was about to receive a major confidence booster. After the summer in Kansas

City, I was invited to speak to a regional gathering of youth groups in Pismo Beach, a coastal community in central California. I didn't know until I arrived that Pismo Beach is a wild place. Surfers and beach bums give it a Star Wars cantina feel. I came expecting to speak to mostly Christian kids in smaller venues and didn't realize the kids were holding public services with music and skits at the pier, drawing thousands of onlookers. I was surprised when the pastor leading the outreach came up to me and said, "In a little while, I want you to close the service. You'll have six minutes in front of this motley crew of people to share the gospel." I looked out at the two or three thousand people standing shoulder to shoulder on the pier and thought, *This is unlike any audience I have spoken to before, and there are so many of them. What am I going to say?*

I had just enough time to run back to my hotel room and fall on my knees.

God, unless you do something through me, this is going to be the biggest flop ever, I prayed. *This crowd is nothing like I've experienced before. And I've got nothing to say to them.*

I didn't get an answer. Heading back to the pier, I clung to the hope that God would intervene somehow—maybe send a sudden rainstorm or make the crowd smaller. From a distance I saw that the crowd was still huge. The great majority seemed to be nonreligious. Chills of fear ran through me. *What in the world am I going to say to these people that will be meaningful?* I asked myself. *Chances are they'll walk away laughing, and I'll ruin everything.*

The moment came. The pastor put the microphone in my hand. I don't recall formulating my thoughts, but somehow the gospel message began to flow out of my mouth. It felt effortless. Words filled my mind, and I felt their power as people listened intently. For those few minutes I felt like an instrument in the hand of almighty God, like a pen used to write his perfect message for those people. When I gave the invitation to receive Jesus, at least a thousand people—more than half the crowd—raised their hands. I felt inspired to say, "If you mean this, if it's a real commitment of your heart, I'm going to meet you down here tomorrow at 9:00 a.m. I'd love to baptize you in the ocean."

I handed the microphone back to the pastor. People were praying with the new converts. It was easily the most powerful moment I had experienced in my short ministry. I went back to my hotel room that night and got on my knees again. *God, that wasn't me,* I prayed. *I don't have the talent or inspiration to pull something like that off.*

Nothing I had ever experienced matched the feeling of partnering with God. Somehow he had used a stuttering, hotheaded sinner like me to share his heavenly message. I was stunned.

The real miracle happened the next day when more than two hundred people returned to be baptized. That's a huge number to come back the next day to be immersed in the chilly Pacific Ocean, and it showed us their conversions were real. A lot of public speakers can influence people through guilt or enthusiasm to raise a hand, but when people wake up the next morning and come back to affirm their change of heart, their confessions are not simply cosmetic.

One woman who looked like she had lived a rough life came into the water with a multicolored parrot on her shoulder.

"Would you baptize my parrot too?" she asked me. I paused a moment, then thought, *What's the harm?* I gave the bird a courtesy dunk, and he came up flapping and flopping as if to say, "What did you do to me?" These people were clearly not stuffy or, for the most part, familiar with church culture. They had come to salvation from all different directions. It was incredibly refreshing.

The feeling on the beach that day was so real. People were hugging and celebrating their decision to follow Jesus. I felt that I had gone out on a limb for God and depended on him for a miracle—and he had delivered, big-time.

A friend once told me, "Luke, you have the gift of evangelism. Some people can speak for hours with little effect, but in about three minutes, you are able to make such a compelling case for giving your life to Christ that people really want to do it." He was right. A gift is something given to you, not something you earn, and I was learning what my gifts were.

And every gift I possessed was about to be tested in Ohio in a crucible that I never saw coming.

2

When Dreams Die

A s I was getting on track with my life purpose, God sent me an Angel—literally.

Angel was a girl I had known since we were teenagers. She was gorgeous and one of the best Christians I'd ever met. We had dated briefly seven years earlier. In fact, her parents had invited me to spend a week with them at their lake house in Idaho, and that's where our relationship ended for the moment. Angel was tough. She had never dated anyone, and from the way she treated me, I wasn't even sure *we* were dating!

On the last day of that vacation, I rode with Angel and her parents to see her horse before we all flew back to Phoenix. The horse saw our vehicle, came up to it, and stuck its head right in. Angel grabbed its muzzle and kissed that thing on the mouth! I couldn't help saying, "That's disgusting." She replied immediately, "I would rather kiss a horse than kiss you."

So ended round one of our relationship. We flew back and went our separate ways.

Angel graduated from high school, went through a ministry training program at our church, then moved to Louisiana to be part of a ministry there. One day her dad was having lunch with my dad and played him a song that Angel had just recorded. My dad was impressed.

"I think Angel would say yes if Luke were to ask her out. What do you think?" Angel's dad asked. Word had gotten around that I was serious about ministry, which is what Angel was looking for in a husband.

Dad came home and played the song for me. I was captivated by the voice.

"Do you know who that is?" Dad asked. "Angel."

"You've got to be kidding me! It's beautiful," I said.

"Yes, she really wants to be in ministry," Dad said. "Here's the deal: her dad says she'll say yes if you ask her out. Do you want to? Because if you don't, I'm going to see if Matthew wants to. I want one of my sons to marry this girl."

Angel and I dated and were married less than a year later. My speaking schedule filled up with dates in Barbados, Hawaii, Singapore, Malaysia, and Bangladesh, so we had a great time seeing the world together. But I soon discovered that everywhere we went I fell in love with the people and wanted to stay and help them grow spiritually. At heart I felt like more of a pastor than an evangelist, so I put out the word that I was interested in being a pastor of a church.

I received exactly one inquiry, from a man in Dayton, Ohio, who had been the pastor of the same church for forty-seven years and was preparing to retire from ministry. There were definite red flags: his church had a hard time keeping youth pastors, music leaders, and other staff positions, and the congregation had shrunk in recent years. I wasn't interested.

But it was as if someone put my phone on silent mode. No one called except for this man in Ohio, who called almost daily. After numerous calls, I agreed to fly out to meet with him.

His church certainly had potential, and when I preached that Sunday, it seemed to go well. Before I left the pastor informed me he was going to stay as copastor and wanted to mentor me.

"Look," I told him, "if you want me to be the pastor, I'll agree to that, but I cannot agree to be the copastor. A two-headed monster is a freak, and it never works. If you're going to stay here, then you need to pastor the church, not me."

He quickly agreed to step down, and within weeks Angel and I moved out to Dayton to lead our first church. I'll give you a few leadership lessons right now: (1) never let the previous pastor stay in your church, (2) always know who owns the property, and (3) keep a crowbar under your car seat in case church life gets rough.

I'm only half-joking.

CONFRONTATION

The church had a beautiful new building with a seating capacity of seven hundred, but fewer than two hundred people were attending at the time. The congregation was very old fashioned and very Pentecostal. People would literally run the aisles screaming and hollering when they got excited. *That's going to have to change,* I thought. I just wasn't that kind of leader.

More to the heart of things, the church was inward looking. By nature and training, I am outward looking, wanting to bless and reach people who don't normally go to church. My goal is to throw open the doors and grow the congregation with new members. Being outward looking is also the best way to avoid internal church conflicts. Outwardly focused people don't have time to fight with each other because they are living to bless others. So I began to change the mind-set and ministry approach by inviting kids and families from the community to attend. I had always been taught by my dad to go to the poorest neighborhoods and try to be a blessing, so we bought four buses and began providing transportation to children in a very poor area of town. We knocked on doors, canvassed the area, and soon had hundreds of kids, mostly African American, coming to church each Sunday.

To my genuine surprise, one Sunday a board member met me at the church door as the kids were running from the buses to the building. "You get those little n—— out of this church," he snarled. "That's not the kind of church we are." The confrontation marked me forever. I saw how religious people and their wicked prejudice get in the way of Jesus's work. I also realized I was on a collision course with some in the church.

In spite of those attitudes, the church grew fast. In just ten months, we were averaging seven hundred people in attendance and added a second morning service. The people of Dayton, Ohio, began talking about what was happening at the church. New people came, hundreds surrendered their lives to God, and nothing short of revival was taking place in that city.

But a certain group of people despised what we were doing and wanted their little church back. They even became violent toward us. During one Wednesday night service, a large man body-slammed my ministry colleague against the wall. I wouldn't have believed it without seeing it. We began to hear threats that they would gun us and our wives down and that we would never leave that city alive. It was like being in a movie, except it was all too real.

The church had previously sued its former denomination for the right to be independent and now belonged to no denomination. The board felt we needed stability and should bring the church into the Assemblies of God. The vote was set for Sunday morning. We had won so many people to the Lord over the past ten months that we believed the vote would be a shoo-in.

The Saturday night before the big vote, I got a call from a board member.

"The old pastor is changing the locks at the church," he said. "He says no one is going to church tomorrow. He claims to own the place."

My father-in-law happened to be in town, so we drove to the church.

The police were there, red and blue lights flashing on their cruiser. The former pastor was there too, and when we approached, we encountered hallways lined with men looking tough and staring us down as we made our way toward the office.

The former pastor and a police officer were there discussing something. My father-in-law, a professional land developer, turned to me. "Luke, let me handle this," he said. "You go out and wait." So I walked back down the hallway, through the intimidating line of guys, and returned to my car. Some of them followed me, surrounded the car, and watched me. I pulled out my phone and called my dad.

"Dad, you won't believe this," I said. "I'm sitting in my car in the church parking lot, and a bunch of guys are standing around like they want to whip me. What do I do?"

"Just stay there," Dad advised immediately. "Lock the doors and don't get out of the car." And people say my dad's not practical!

Finally, the police officer and my father-in-law came out. The officer said, "The man owns the building. He can do what he wants."

The board members went home and made flyers that explained why the church was locked down. The next morning, my heart broke as I watch brand-new followers of Jesus drive up to a locked church. Board members stood in the street near the church and handed out the flyers inviting people to go to the Holiday Inn later that night for an explanation of what had happened. That night, five hundred people showed up at the Holiday Inn; many of them had come to Christ within the past year under our ministry. Angel and I looked at each other and knew we couldn't leave these people without a shepherd. Though it was never our intention, we were about to become church planters.

We started a church in a nearby town and soon outgrew first the ballroom at the hotel and next the elementary school auditorium we'd been renting. We eventually bought a property with seventy-two thousand square feet of building space, plenty of offices, and lots of parking. Even though God gave us great favor and growth, I still questioned deeply why he had moved us into such a difficult situation. We endured four very painful years, and I often had to heed the message I preached: do a good job before your dream job. I knew that unless I put my shoulder into the work and stuck with it, I would begin to drift from my life purpose.

If we don't find joy in the journey, none of us will reach our dreams. The Bible says that the joy of the Lord is our strength (see Nehemiah 8:10). If we are not joyful, we won't have the strength and stamina to complete our journeys. Joy is an indicator of strength. They always go hand in hand.

I often strengthened myself by thinking of other people's journeys, including my dad's. One time when we were kids, Dad drove us through the Armourdale neighborhood in Kansas City where he grew up. I was shocked by what I saw: dilapidated buildings, crumbling streets, tumble-down houses.

"Was it like this when you lived here?" I asked.

"Yes, it was," Dad said. "But we didn't know it was the ghetto, and the ghetto didn't get in us."

Dad overcame that situation and became a world-renowned evange-list when he was just sixteen years old. He preached to people including Elvis Presley and Colonel Sanders of Kentucky Fried Chicken, and he even produced a movie shot on location around the world. At thirty-one he announced that he wanted to pastor a church, but nobody would take him because they believed that evangelists couldn't be successful pastors. The only open door was at a little church in Davenport, Iowa, which seated about a hundred people. As Dad recalls it, they were the meanest Christians he had ever seen in his life.

He was so embarrassed by the church that he wouldn't even invite his friends to come preach. But he planted his life there and brought the hurting, the lost, the poor, and those with special needs to church. God blessed it greatly, and in nine years it became the fastest growing church in America. Four thousand people attended on weekends. It was the talk of the nation. Johnny Cash was so impressed by Dad's heart that he offered to come and do a concert in Davenport. He sang, Dad preached, and they shared the gospel at John O'Donnell Stadium. Thirty-five thousand people showed up, and more than five thousand gave their hearts to Jesus. In fact, Cash wrote a song called "Billy and Rex and Oral and Bob" that mentioned my dad's name.

In 1979 Dad got a call from a church in Phoenix that was notorious for devouring pastors. It had gone through ten pastors in about ten years. People told him, "You can't do the kind of ministry here that you did in Davenport. Phoenix is a white-collar area. Rich people want to worship God with rich people, poor people with poor people." Dad didn't buy that. He began to reach out to people no other church wanted. He bought buses to bring special-needs people and the poor to church. The church grew from 250 people to fifteen thousand, becoming one of the first megachurches in modern America. He later started the Los Angeles Dream Center in downtown LA, and it has inspired and equipped millions of people worldwide and become a beacon of hope.

Even if Dayton wasn't my dream job, I knew that Dad and others had gone through equally hard times in their assignments. I also knew that hidden in difficult situations are the tests that lead to our next promotion. If I wanted to go forward in health and strength, I had to be faithful with what I had been given and keep my joy.

Go West

By 1999 the Dayton church was the talk of pastors around the nation. They were excited to see a young Barnett out there church planting and growing a congregation. For me, it was a validation of the way my dad had always done ministry, because we were employing his strategies and principles. I was proud to be involved in it.

But when I got a call from a church in Southern California, I was ready to say yes, with some convincing. The pastor there was also retiring and began calling me regularly. "We'd love you to come here and be our pastor," he told me. "We're a well-established church. I've been here thirty-five years, but we're in a little bit of decline. We need some fresh leadership."

The church was located in the Los Angeles area, in a community that had once been mostly white but was now 90 percent Hispanic. The congregation, however, was still almost entirely white. People were driving in from other neighborhoods to continue attending, and the church was not reaching the nearby community. If its leaders stuck with their present strategy, the church would get smaller and more insular.

After much prayer, Angel and I felt good about this move, so we left Dayton and took the helm of this congregation of four hundred. The property was badly showing its age. Peach-colored wallpaper greeted us in some rooms, along with green carpets, old pews, and lots of deferred maintenance. One thing the church had always poured a lot of energy into was their fifty-voice choir, which wore robes, and a big orchestra that played excellently. The only downside was that the choir and orchestra no longer reflected or connected with the nearby community, and the style of music was growing outdated.

When a new pastor comes to town, there is always interest, and the church experienced an immediate growth spurt. We added a second service, and within six months attendance had doubled. The church seemed to be coming back to life, and for the first time we were reaching families who lived nearby. But to my true disappointment, I heard comments from church members who didn't want Hispanic people coming to their church. I had figured, wrongly I guess, that westerners were more progressive in their acceptance of other cultures. As happy as I was about the health and growth that was happening, my soul was dismayed by that response.

Still, I thought we could all grow together through the changes, and things were going so well that we decided to start a Saturday evening service to reach younger people. Instead of having the choir sing, I wanted to bring in a young worship leader to give this service a more contemporary feel. I should have known I was picking a fight, because the present worship leader was the former pastor's son-in-law, and the former pastor—you guessed it—was still attending the church. So began an ugly rift. The former pastor, who was a good man, began to turn against my leadership. At first when longtime members came to him to complain about me, he said, "Oh, let's support him." Then it became, "I wouldn't do it that way, but let's support him." Then after a little more time, it turned into, "Yeah, he's not doing it our way."

Before I knew it, he had started a "Bible study" two blocks away. His son-in-law left his position as the worship leader at our church, and hundreds of members followed him. The Sunday after their departure, our church looked like a ghost town. There was a clear racial motivation as well. Some people had dug in their heels and protested about reaching out to the community and "bringing that riffraff into the church," as one member put it. Ugh.

As in Dayton, we essentially started over with the three hundred remaining people and a budget one quarter of what it had been before. *Here we go again,* I thought.

At that point I slipped into a sort of numbness. Five years of church planting after the initial crazy circumstance in Ohio had worn down our emotions and our bodies. We had hoped the California church would be a little more straightforward, but now we were going through the same thing—just with better weather.

I found myself spending long nights driving around Los Angeles, heading out to the beach, thinking and talking to God until the sun rose.

This is so painful, God, I said. *What are you doing to me? I'm just trying to be obedient. This is not what I had in mind when I followed your call on my life. I can't live the rest of my life feeling like everything is falling apart and it's all on me to fix it.*

For the first time I began to have real doubts about my future in ministry. I simply didn't want to fight anymore. I had been plowing away for more than a decade, and the excitement and confidence from early on had long since ebbed away. I was leading as best I could from my natural gifts, but the joy was gone. Sheer tenacity kept me in the game. One of our family slogans is that Barnetts aren't quitters. I heard my dad's voice echo that phrase over and over in my head. But I had gone from battle to battle without rest, and even though God was blessing the church and we were starting to grow again, it almost didn't matter because I was so beaten down emotionally.

What in the world am I doing? Nothing seems to be working, I thought while driving through random neighborhoods. *I feel like I'm spinning my wheels. I can't fathom going through life like this. There's got to be an easier way.*

During that time I deeply examined my eleven years of ministry. Really, I had done exactly what I had seen my dad do so well and for so long—throwing open the doors to the community, busing in the needy and poor, reaching out to every hurting person. The more I thought about it, the more those things felt like someone else's vision—incredibly godly and amazing but not springing from my own soul. Those things were my father's dream, and I believed in his dream, but it wasn't totally satisfying to me at a deep heart level. I knew I had something of my own to contribute—but what?

I thought about the times I had felt God's wind at my back—on the pier in Pismo Beach, at a particular conference in Russia where God moved in an amazing way, and a few other times. Those moments felt powerful, important, uplifting. By comparison, 99 percent of the ministry I did felt man-made, like a job I hated going to. If it was God's work, where was the feeling of blessing? Where was that supernatural wind at my back from time to time?

I heard reports of how other churches were thriving and growing. Their ministries seemed exciting, their vision fresh. Something was missing from my life and ministry, but I didn't know what.

WHY DREAMERS KEEP GOING

I had always studied dreamers and difference makers, people like my dad, Billy Graham, Bill Bright, and Bill Hybels. What was going on in their hearts before they held their first big stadium meeting or started a church or a world-changing ministry? What prompted them to dream that big?

My conclusion was different from what you might expect. I came to believe that these men were driven not by a positive vision but rather by a firestorm experience, an abiding frustration that catapulted them into their cause. Moses of the Old Testament is a good example. People think it was the awe of that burning bush that catapulted Moses into his cause. But I think the bush was just a reminder of a much earlier memory. Forty years earlier he left the palace where he lived to visit his people, the Jews. He saw an Egyptian beating a Jew. The beating was so violent and bloody that the sights and sounds of it marked Moses forever. He couldn't stand it anymore. "He looked this way and that, and seeing no one, he struck down the Egyptian and hid him in the sand" (Exodus 2:12).

That scene of suffering and oppression pushed him to his emotional limits. Forty years later when he stood before the burning bush, that same feeling—the sights and sounds of that horrible beating—remained in his heart. The burning bush was an attention grabber to slow him down to listen to his own heart again. What God said from the burning bush resonated inside Moses. "I have surely seen the affliction of my people who are in Egypt" (Exodus 3:7). In other words, "Moses, I saw and heard what you saw and heard. I can't take it anymore either. You and I are stirred in our hearts for the very same things. We can't stand idly by. I see in you my own burning desire for justice. I'm going to harness that firestorm of frustration inside you and use it in a positive way to set my people free."

In the same way, you and I become difference makers when our hearts align with God's heart around a cause that frustrates both of us.

David had a divine dissatisfaction as well. He delivered lunch to his brothers on the front lines of battle and heard a nasty giant blaspheming the God David loved. "Isn't anyone going to do something?" David asked, but the soldiers weren't nearly as repulsed as David was. Irrationally, David went up against that giant with nothing but a sling, stones, and raw passion (see 1 Samuel 17). Where was the business plan in that? There was none, but David's heart was aligned with God's, and the power flowed to accomplish the great task.

My dad was driven by frustration that certain people in society aren't reached by most churches. So he did something about it wherever he went. I believe he left a significant mark on the church worldwide because of that divine dissatisfaction.

Where was my dissatisfaction? What was I frustrated about? What couldn't I ignore anymore? The truth was—not much. My early passion for souls was still there, but my hope was trampled by all the battles we had fought. I didn't know how to say it then, but I was living without a dream. I couldn't see a positive vision of my future. Yes, people were blessed week after week, but something was missing in my own heart. Nothing fired me up anymore.

On the outside, things looked fine. We held three morning services with twelve hundred people attending on weekends. We had a debt-free building with a renovated auditorium, new carpets and paint, theater seats, and a café. The church was now 90 percent Hispanic, and I considered that a great victory—it belonged to the community again. By all visible metrics we had successfully bounced back. But I was secretly entertaining ways to leave ministry without being viewed as a quitter. I had no dream for it. I was done.

One day, God nudged me and said simply, *Your time here is done. I have a new assignment for you.* He didn't reveal what the assignment was. I just sensed a prompting to go.

Honestly, relief washed over me, mixed with disappointment that I still hadn't found my passion.

God, what's the next assignment? I asked.

He gave no answer. But I knew it was time to step down from the church.

Just before going into the board meeting to announce my departure, I called my dad to tell him.

"What do you think?" I asked.

"Don't do it, Son," he said. "Wait for something to open up."

I considered his words and remembered the clear nudge from my heavenly Father.

"Dad, I love you, but I think I've heard from God on this," I said. "I appreciate your wisdom, but I think God is asking me to step out alone on this one."

I walked into the meeting, and the board members were shocked to hear my news. They hadn't seen it coming at all. I understood. I tend to look upbeat no matter how I'm feeling. They questioned why I was leaving right when things were going well. All I could tell them was that my passion had lifted for this area, and God had made it evident that he was moving me on. Thankfully, God also made it clear to all of us that the associate pastor, my best friend, Dave Ansell, should step into the senior pastor role.

The transition was wonderfully smooth, and the people were very understanding, but Angel and I didn't know what to do next. Heaven was silent. We decided it was best to move back to Phoenix near family to wait on God for what was ahead. I began speaking at churches around the world and consulting with churches to share some of our hard-won knowledge as they navigated their own difficulties.

Part of me was hoping for a graceful exit from full-time ministry and an open door to something else.

I wanted a different dream.

3

A Rising Son
in Phoenix

Luke, we would like you to join the staff of this church as the executive pastor."

The invitation caught me totally by surprise and troubled me because it was from my dad's church.

"Does my dad know about this?" I asked immediately.

"Yes," said the board member. "We had to convince him of it. He's not one to hire his kids."

I laughed inwardly—that was certainly true. Dad preferred to send us to the University of Hard Knocks, and I felt as though I had earned a doctorate degree over the past twelve years.

Angel and I and our two daughters had moved back to Phoenix four months earlier, with no intention of taking a position at the church. We just wanted to hole up in a safe place and figure out the future. During that time, Dad often asked me to preach and teach. It was a very busy ministry season for him. He was doing a lot of traveling to raise funds to support the Los Angeles Dream Center, and since I was in Phoenix, I was his go-to teacher when he was gone. I didn't expect my work at the church to go beyond that, but when we reflected on it, it seemed right. After praying and talking about it, I let the board and Dad know I would accept the invitation, with one ultimatum: "When my dad leaves, I leave,"

I told the board. "His last day here is my last day here. I'm not coming to expedite my dad's exit. I'm here to support him."

"We appreciate and respect that," they said.

Moving back to Phoenix and coming on staff happened so fast I almost had whiplash. Suddenly I was in a position I never expected to be in—helping to lead the massive church I had grown up in with its many amazing ministries. As a pastor's kid, I tended to take my surroundings for granted. Now I looked around at everything going on at Phoenix First and found it more than a little daunting.

It reminded me of the day when I was nineteen and a group of NBA players came to our church for an athletes' conference. A little background: one of the church's more than 250 ministries was called Athletes International Ministry. The dream for this ministry started in the heart of a man named Larry Kerychuk. Larry sat in my living room when I was a little boy and talked to my dad about this wild vision of having the greatest athletes from around the world come to an annual conference and be built up in their faith. Larry was another of the dreamers I knew as I grew up, and so many of the dreams I saw then, including Larry's, have become reality.

The conference hosted leaders such as boxing legend Evander Holyfield, NBA hall of famer David Robinson, NFL legend Larry Fitzgerald, and MLB hall of famer Rickey Henderson. The list could go on and on. During the conference, some of the collegiate and NBA players had some free time and said, "Let's go play some hoops." I was volunteering as the athletics coordinator at the time, and my brother, Matthew, and I were always hanging around the gym playing basketball. The players started to assemble—Brent Price, who played for a number of NBA teams and was the brother of Cleveland Cavaliers point guard Mark Price; Wayman Tisdale, who played a dozen years in the NBA; David Wood, who played nine years in the NBA; plus a bunch of college Division I players hoping to make the pros soon. I could hardly believe my eyes. They didn't act like privileged professionals; instead, they seemed like a bunch of schoolkids who just wanted to play.

"Hey, we need some extra players," they said as they divided into teams, and just like that, Matthew and I were added to their ranks.

Incredible! I thought. *Now I get to see what I'm really made of.*

Though I stood just five foot nine and Matthew five foot ten, we didn't lack confidence. We were winning city leagues and playing at parks and gyms around the area. Like arrogant teenagers, we thought we could hang with anyone.

That proved a little naive. As the game got underway, I felt overwhelmed by my opponents' sheer size. They were so tall, with arms like tree branches and hands the size of dinner plates. When they pressed me, their arms seemed to wrap around my body, and their size filled my field of vision.

There's no way I'll get anything past these guys, I thought, dribbling to save my life.

There was no audience to impress, and it was nothing more than a pickup game at a church gymnasium, but everyone's juices were up from the start. The college guys wanted to impress the NBA guys, and the NBA guys didn't want to look bad in front of each other. One guy put up a shot and another swatted it out of bounds. "Get out of my house!" he said. I thought, *This isn't even your house.*

As the shortest and least experienced player on our team, I played point guard. Under normal playing conditions, I didn't have to worry about someone stealing the ball because I had pretty good ball-handling skills. But these guys were so quick that I had to spend all my energy and focus guarding the ball. At any moment they could reach around and snatch it away. In normal circumstances I often shot from the outside, and I fancied myself a good outside shooter. But the idea of getting a shot off against these guys was laughable. Matthew, too, was a good slasher against normal opponents. He would drive in, use his body to bounce off people, pull attention to himself, then pass the ball to me, and I would make the shot. But he, too, was almost completely stifled. None of our usual magic worked. I remember glancing at him and knowing our roles had to change. I even found it a challenge to do a simple thing like dribble the ball up the court and find someone to pass to.

About halfway through the ninety-minute game, my mind seemed to catch up a little bit. I started seeing small cracks in the defense that I thought about exploiting with a pass or an alley-oop. Scoring was out of the question, but I could try to feed the ball to the pros. One time I was brave enough to actually throw an alley-oop toward the basket. One of our guys grabbed it midair and slammed it into the basket for a dunk. He landed and looked at me in a way that said, *Nice job, little guy. Not bad for a preacher's kid.*

From that point on I began to see more open spaces to pass the ball so the big guys could make a play. In a small way I surprised myself, seeing that I could benefit my team though I'd never played at any college level.

Becoming the executive pastor at Dad's church, I felt the same way. I had never considered working at a place like Phoenix First because it was so world class that I didn't think I could contribute much. Also, it operated differently than the churches I led in Ohio and California. It was fueled by Dad's vision and calling. All he had to say was, "Folks, we're going this way. Everybody jump on board and let's go!" And it worked. If I tried that, people would say, "Uh, let me think about that." I had nowhere near his charm and vision. I felt like the point guard feeding him the ball so he could score.

In truth, I was amazed just to be on the team. I spent the first months working hard to support my dad, building up the ministries of the church, improving the already-great children's program, hiring awesome youth leaders, strengthening our church community. Soon I was teaching every Wednesday evening and organizing the midweek service. Then I was teaching every Sunday night and sharing pulpit time on Sunday mornings.

Then God threw us a curveball.

My dad played lunchtime basketball with the young staff members every Monday and Tuesday until he was seventy-three. He was very competitive, and what he lacked in quickness and jumping ability, he made up with dirty tactics. One day he began to experience shortness of breath. The doctors discovered that Dad's heart valve needed repair. They would have to open him up; recovery time could be more than six months. Suddenly, my reintegration into church life, which had been going along at a normal pace, was on fast-forward. I was surprised to learn from the board and Dad that they wanted me to lead the church in the interim while Dad recovered.

The people at Phoenix First had known me as a kid and a young man, still rough around the edges. While I was a pastor elsewhere, Dad had bragged on me for years. He told stories about our struggles and victories in Ohio and Southern California. He turned Matthew's and my little triumphs into the world's greatest achievements. He painted me in such a good light that the people probably thought I could walk on water. I'm glad they never asked for a demonstration.

One Sunday, Dad stood before the congregation and explained what the next few months would look like.

"I have to have heart-valve surgery," he told the people, "so I have asked Luke to lead the church while I recover. It could be three months or nine months. I'm not a young man. Right now I'm asking you to be supportive of Luke. I have asked him to lead this church as he would if I were dead. I don't want him to base decisions on the way I would do it. I want him to be led by God."

That was true. Dad had told me repeatedly and firmly, "Do not do church the way I do. You do things as if I were dead and gone. You're in charge. Do the sermons and series you want. Do the lights and music the way you want. We're going to let God be God."

The people embraced the plan, and on Valentine's Day Dad had a successful heart surgery. As we walked through his recovery together, I figured we would find out pretty quickly if my leadership had any future at the church. None of us knew how the people would respond with me temporarily at the helm.

I spent hours privately assessing my leadership style during those days and weeks. In a number of ways, I am the opposite of my dad. My personality is different, to begin with. I'm organizationally minded and enjoy the nuts and bolts of administration. Dad is all about the big picture. He speaks to people's desire to achieve great things. He can mobilize thousands with a single message. I didn't feel I had that tool in my belt. Rather than inspiring people from the pulpit, I had developed a more face-to-face, personal style of leadership. I grabbed lunch and dinner with people, had meetings, coffees, relationship-building times. I talked a lot about community and doing church together as a team. My way wasn't better, but I was using the strength I had.

Dad was enthusiastic about any level of success, while I tended to see the one small thing that was wrong. He didn't care to know attendance numbers. I wanted every metric I could find to see how we were doing this year compared to last. Dad wasn't concerned about that at all, as long as people were catching the vision. Without placing a value judgment on our different ways of doing things, I began to note the contrasts and how they might hinder or help my leadership at the church.

For the time being, we were all in a holding pattern while Dad got well. I didn't cast vision but just fed the flock in normal ways: teaching, doing sermon series I felt would build people up, being creative with the arts during our services. We all felt like we were rallying around the general while he was down.

Within a few weeks I felt that things were clicking. There was a fresh wind in the place, and it wasn't due to my leadership. Within just three months we saw a 20 percent increase in our attendance and weekly financial support. It was obvious God was up to something, but we didn't know quite what. Maybe he was just affirming the church during Dad's downtime.

It took a fresh set of eyes to see clearly. Five months after the surgery, Dad came back and sat in the front row. Much had changed. The church had grown dramatically. Some new people even greeted him in the parking lot and said, "Hello, sir. Are you a first-time visitor? Can I point you to the auditorium?"

Of course, on an atmospheric level, he didn't like everything he saw. For example, the lights were now kept low in the main sanctuary. Dad preferred every light bulb burning at full wattage so he could see people's eyeballs. However, the small, personal preferences paled in comparison to what he experienced that day in church. Dad loved what he saw happening.

"I don't even recognize this church," he told me afterward. "Lives are changing and this place is growing. Luke, this church is no longer mine, it's yours. It has moved forward. You are the man. I knew I could never give you this church. I knew the people had to speak—and they have. So many pastors get in trouble when they try to give their son the church. It just doesn't work. But I think God has been transitioning us all these years without our even knowing it. We have to move ahead with this transition right now."

I was seeing the same evidence he was seeing, but it was still hard for me to imagine leading the church, and my dad not leading it. His plan was always to die in the pulpit. "You don't quit on God," he often said.

But it seemed now that God had forced change on us so that Dad wouldn't have to hold to that promise.

"I'm moving to LA," Dad continued. "I'm going to get out of your hair. It wouldn't be right for me to stay because of my legacy here. I want you to have a clear field to lead."

"Dad, don't go," I told him. "You need to stay here. I need you here. I need your influence. Why don't you keep the title of senior pastor and I'll become the lead pastor. And if you will give me the opportunity to lead, we can work together. However, you have to allow me to lead."

It was so refreshing to hear someone offer to bow out, after my previous experiences in Ohio and California, but the last thing I wanted was for him to leave. Finally, I convinced him to stay, and we went to the board with the plan. One board member started crying when we described the transition.

"We love you so much, Tommy," he said. "You are such a dynamic leader, and we have wondered for years how this church could go on without you. Only God could provide for us a five-month window to give us assurance that this church will move forward and stay strong under new leadership." I'll never forget that historic meeting.

It was decided: I would become the lead pastor while Dad would retain the senior pastor title. We kept this system in place from June 2011 until the summer of 2013. It went well and the church grew. However, Dad began traveling the world, teaching and encouraging other pastors. He was gone so much that we couldn't have our regular board meetings. As the senior pastor, Dad was the chairman of the church board, which meant we couldn't have meetings while he was gone. Finally, Dad said, "Luke, we need to make you the senior pastor so the church can move forward and be healthy and not be dependent on my schedule."

So we officially passed the baton of ministry in June of 2013. I was excited, but I had no idea I was about to encounter an onslaught of the

Enemy's discouragement that would nearly drive me from my assignment before it got off the ground.

THE BATON AND THE FAST

Dad proved his character over and over again as we headed toward an official transfer of leadership.

"People are going to say, 'Back in Tommy's day things were so good,'" he warned me. "Don't you listen to them. Things have never been bigger and better than they are right now. These are the good ol' days."

He became my head cheerleader and personal coach. At times I focused on negatives, and he gave me an actual tongue-lashing on a couple of occasions.

"This church has never been as healthy as it is right now," he said more than once. "We're at a whole other level. You need to repent, Luke. You're ungrateful. God has been so good to us. You're focusing on the negative. If you can't see what God is doing, you're blind."

That's how Barnetts encourage one another!

The Sunday of the official transition rolled around, and I stood there with one arm around Dad and the other around Angel. Mom stood with us. Dad passed the golden baton of ministry, symbolizing all the work he had done in nearly six decades, and I gratefully accepted it. Tears filled my eyes as I told the people, "I'm no Tommy Barnett. God has used him to do amazing things in his lifetime. To the best of my abilities, I'll live a life of integrity and generosity, and I'll love you with all my heart. We'll trust God to do the great exploits through us. You know I'm not a crier."

Dad broke in, "It's the first time I've seen you cry. You do have a heart!"

With that, I became the leader of Phoenix First Assembly. And without any warning whatsoever, I walked off an emotional cliff.

I can't explain how it began except to say that a blanket of depression came upon me that was far beyond anything I had ever experienced. The lies assaulting my mind felt like a constant bombardment.

You'll never be able to fill the shoes you're stepping into. They're way too big for you.

You can't inspire people like your dad did. This church is dead in the water with you leading it.

You don't have what it takes to rise to this occasion. You were lucky to get this far.

The people aren't going to follow you. After a while everyone is going to just drift away. You'll preside over the death of this place.

The sudden onslaught made no sense. Outwardly, nothing had really changed. The previous two years as lead pastor had been smooth and actually quite encouraging. I had been serving in the role of senior pastor with the title of lead pastor. Really, nothing had changed. Angel and I felt blessed and relaxed to be back home. We had a strong community around us and felt accepted and supported. Our kids were thriving and happy. But the moment I officially took leadership, it was as if someone flipped a switch in my thought life. Immediately I felt like giving up. I lost interest in the work. I felt insufficient, incapable, inexplicably tired all the time. The burden was so heavy that I didn't think I could carry it for very long.

I kept this fact from Angel for a while. I prefer to internalize things rather than drag her down. I didn't want her or the people in the church to know their leader was feeling down. I brought it up with Dad a couple of times, but he just encouraged me even more: "You're doing great. You're amazing." Those answers felt almost shallow. He is such an amazing encourager, but I didn't want encouragement—I wanted help!

None came, at least not immediately. I continued going to work and slugging it out but felt miserable and completely uninterested. My lack of excitement bothered me greatly. So did my fear of failure. Living in Dad's shadow had never haunted me before. I had always been secure in my strengths and talents. Now I began to seriously entertain the idea that I was the wrong guy to take this church forward. Maybe I wasn't gifted for it or up to the challenge. I certainly didn't want to just take a paycheck. It made me sick to think of maintaining Dad's church without seeing God do something new and great. We are supposed to go from glory to glory, higher and higher in our life purposes. I had to see something big happen in my lifetime, or no effort would be worth it.

I often chided myself: *What are you complaining about, anyway? Our church is experiencing great things that other churches only dream about. We have reached our promised land compared to so many.* But I knew there was more we had not experienced. Angel and I had enjoyed a number of good seasons in ministry, but we seldom had felt the surge of God pushing the work forward, his obvious presence partnering with us. More often it was about staying in the battle, putting our hands to the plow every day. I hate to say it, but much of the ministry I had done up to then felt like it was done in the flesh.

This was especially embarrassing because I've always been surrounded by dreamers: my dad, my brother, Larry Kerychuk, Sharon Henning, Dr. Rahman, and hundreds of other dreamers at our church. It seemed that all those around me were natural dreamers and visionaries who inspired others just by speaking what was in their hearts. I view myself as more of a teacher and administrator. I can run an organization pretty well, but it was a dream that built Phoenix First from a five-acre campus to a seventy-two acre campus, from a small local church to a world-influencing juggernaut. A dream had done the same thing with a small congregation in Los Angeles, which became the Dream Center movement. Dad's vision for new things was so white hot, so compelling, that he lived in a constant state of enthusiasm—and the results were simply incredible.

To be truthful, the idea of leading from a dream had bothered me at times. In the past, I'd sort of pooh-poohed having a big dream. I was more interested in setting achievable goals, hitting deadlines and targets, managing people, and taking a steady upward journey. I probably discounted the importance of dreaming big because I didn't understand it. Dreams weren't necessary in the positions I was in. Rather, I put my head down and worked. It wasn't always exciting, but it yielded results.

The problem, I began to see, is that people can go only so far without a God-sized dream propelling them forward. The fact that I was following one of the great dreamers on the planet but didn't have my own dream scared me. I had witnessed the power of a dream my whole life. Yet I had never paid the price to get a God-sized dream for myself. I now was at the highest leadership level, operating on my dad's dream and methods. That's like finding yourself ten thousand feet in the air with feathers taped to your arms. It wasn't going to work.

In the midst of that confusion, God made one thing clear to me: I really wasn't fit for the job if I didn't have a dream. I didn't need to become my dad, but I needed to discover the dream that would inspire me and the people I was leading. I said to God, *That's true. That's what's missing in my life—something so exciting and compelling that it will fire me up every day for the rest of my life. Who wouldn't die for a vision like that? I have to hear from you. I need a firsthand revelation. I know I need to go all-in. Take me on a journey to find my dream.*

This time of oppression lasted two months, my thoughts swirling, my doubts getting the upper hand almost every day. I believe it was spiritual. I think Satan was doing everything in his power to derail the dream before it started. He wanted me out of the game because if I ever locked into God's inspired dream for me, something dramatic could happen.

A LIFE-CHANGING FAST

I was ready to do something bold and dramatic to break out of the oppression—but what?

My mind went to my dad's lifelong habit of grabbing his newspaper and Bible every morning and climbing the mountain behind the church to spend time with God. In fact, when I was an eighteen-year-old kid, I worked at the church during the summer and drove the Bobcat tractor up the mountain, cleared the space, and graded the ground that my dad would pray on for many years. It was a small dirt platform perfect for pacing. He even installed a safe in the rocks and stashed a Bible there so he wouldn't have to carry it up every day. Some days he was there thirty minutes; some days it was two hours. He imagined that Jesus was right next to him, sitting in the empty chair, reading the newspaper with him, and having coffee. He spoke to God like they were close friends. Dad's dreams were born in those times when he looked over the city of Phoenix and imagined what could be.

I knew prayer would be part of my breakthrough.

My friend Jentezen Franklin, a pastor in Georgia, had started doing a month of prayer and fasting every year with his church. I listened to a message he preached about it and was very inspired. Jentezen's church is phenomenal and his preaching is powerful. I could almost feel the heat of his words warming my cold heart again. I knew that nothing would happen unless I was hungry enough to pursue God's dream for me in a radical way. What was more radical than going without food?

So, with no fanfare and only a brief public announcement, I started a forty-day Daniel fast, the first extended fast of my life. Anything that grew directly from the ground and was not from an animal, I could eat. And Starbucks coffee. That was my one cheat.

I made "prayer mountain" behind the church my second home. Dad's most recent major ministry accomplishment in Phoenix had been the Prayer Pavilion built on the side of the mountain behind our church. It's a beautiful structure made mostly of glass and built on concrete stilts thirty feet high. Two massive bronze doors with the Lord's Prayer engraved on them greet you at the entrance. Large glass doors open up to a balcony overlooking the city. Below, a large landscaped prayer garden shows off cacti, flowers, and desert plants. It's open round the clock but is especially beautiful at night when the city lights are twinkling and the side of the mountain is lit up like a lantern with hundreds of LED lights.

Dad had fought hard to get the Prayer Pavilion built, overcoming fierce opposition from some people who represented the city of Phoenix. Interestingly, it was the last thing he saw in his vision for ministry in Phoenix. Beyond that he had no dream. Now the pavilion became the place where a new vision for the church was being born.

Every morning at 5:30 or so, I took the paved walkway up to the pavilion. Sometimes I continued on one of the paths behind the pavilion where the ground gets steep and the path splits into a dozen directions, each created by someone seeking God's answer. More often I went into the pavilion itself. The soft, beautiful music that plays continuously in the building injected peace into my soul.

God, give me a dream.

I prayed it over and over, and then I sat quietly and listened. After a while I went down the hill to work. The next day I made the climb again.

God, give me a dream.

The hunger pangs were there, but I also felt a surprising spiritual and mental alertness. My teaching and preaching were sharper, more powerful. I had more physical energy than I expected. Hunger pangs reminded me of my purpose.

God, give me a dream.

Soon, thoughts started coming to mind. As I looked over the city, I thought about our church. What were we good at? What did we enjoy doing? I began to feel the impressions and whispers of God. His attention seemed to rest on five specific areas of a dream he had for our church. I never heard his audible voice, but I felt consistent nudges in certain directions. The nudges became so persistent that soon it was all I could think about. All day long, in the midst of other tasks, I dwelled on the five things that filled my mind and how they might work. Each component was so powerful I knew it was from outside myself. I had never felt so much inspiration and quiet confidence in a specific direction. I knew I was receiving the vision that would fire me up for the rest of my life.

The first thing God whispered to me was that our church would become the arts hub of Arizona. That was the furthest thing from my mind when I began the fast. I'm not particularly artistic, though I love the arts, and I know how much energy, time, and money dramatic presentations take. Each year, our drama team starts rehearsals in August for the Christmas show, which involves a cast and crew of a thousand people. Seventy-five thousand people attend the sixteen performances. Over the past thirty-five years, nearly two million people in the greater Phoenix area have experienced the *Celebration of Christmas* production. To increase the number of theatrical shows we did throughout the year seemed a real stretch.

Yet it also fit our history. Dad had always used dramatic presentations the way his hero, Aimee Semple McPherson, and his own mother, Joy

Barnett, had done. The reason our church has two balconies is because it's patterned after McPherson's Angelus Temple in Los Angeles and the Grand Ole Opry in Nashville. From the time I was a kid, dramatic presentations were a big deal at our church, especially at Christmas and Easter. Often, Dad preached illustrated sermons that involved actors, laser lights, fog, pyrotechnics, even flying angels. It was bred in me from an early age!

Now I sensed that God wanted the church to go to an entirely new level. He wanted everyone in the entire state to look to us as the premier, go-to place for training and participating in the arts. He wanted us to put on Broadway-quality shows and summer musicals and bring people from all over the state to our campus as we built bridges to people in the arts community.

It was a huge idea for me. Sometimes you know a dream is from God because there's no way you would have had the courage to dream it up yourself.

Second, God told me he would use our church to train one hundred thousand pastors and leaders through our annual Dream Conference over the next ten years. Our conferences for pastors had always drawn thousands of people from all over, but now I saw that God had an even brighter vision for those events. It would be a whole new day in training leaders from around the world.

Third, he gave me a vision for an $8 million extension to the church building to include a brand-new lobby and children's facilities—and told me we would be completely debt free by 2023, the church's one hundredth birthday. That perplexed me more than excited me. I had no idea how we would accomplish that, so I accepted it by faith. But I saw no path forward.

Fourth, he let me know he wanted a greater emphasis on small groups, and he put a number in my mind: fifty thousand people attending five thousand small groups all across the state of Arizona. Again, I was staggered by the scope of the vision, but I knew his purpose was in it.

Fifth, and perhaps most shocking, he wanted us to become a multi-site campus, and he showed me how we would reach our entire state. In the same way Utah is known for being a Mormon state, California is known as a center for entertainment, and New York is known for business and finance, God wanted Arizona to be known as a Christian state. He showed me it would be popular one day for young people to become worship leaders, youth pastors, senior pastors, and more and that our church would raise them up and launch them all across the state. Part of the strategy was having sites in different cities, such as Tucson, Prescott, Yuma, and Flagstaff. God wanted us to help him wrap the state in his love.

The impressions were so strong, and my passion so kindled by them, that I knew I would never get tired of the five-point vision God had given me. At the same time, it just about scared me to death.

To Share or Not to Share

When God gives a dream, he doesn't often give details. I had tons of questions as I continued the fast. What kind of risk would it be for us as a church to actually attempt these things? What toll would it take on my family? Where would the resources come from? Where would the people come from? How would we sustain it? What if everything fell flat?

As I continued to climb the mountain and pray, I wrestled with one question in particular: *Should I share the vision with the people?*

I felt a powerful temptation to shut the door on what God had shown me. In a sense, I had already arrived. I was the leader now. I could spend the next twenty-five years being the nice little pastor of the megachurch on the mountain, shepherding the flock, staying in familiar territory, not challenging myself or anyone else. When faced with a vision the size God was giving me, comfort seemed an attractive option.

I thought of the battles that lay between us and the fulfillment of the vision. Financial battles, battles over misunderstanding and changes, battles over the nature of the vision and how it should get done. A thousand different challenges seemed to jeer at me from various corners of my imagination. Did I really want to deal with any of them?

The dangerous thing about nudges from God is that they are inherently private. Nobody knows about them except you and God. You have the choice to ignore them, and nobody will say you are being disobedient or unspiritual. In truth, people usually say you're being sensible when you choose not to dream big. Dreamers are often called arrogant, impractical. People ask, "Who do you think you are to dream like that?" In reality it's not who we are but who God is that compels us to dream. When God calls us to possess the land, it is no small thing—and the vision doesn't come from us but from him.

As I had often heard and preached, secret faith is shallow faith, and with the dream burning in my heart, I knew I had to share it. I did this first with the people around me—my wife, my dad, close staff members and ministry associates—and then more publicly. It was the only way to see if the dream resonated with others, to see if they were willing to sacrifice for it like I was. I knew that the moment the vision was out of my mouth, people would start mobilizing. Networking would begin to happen. A dream is powerless when it's inside someone. It becomes powerful only when released into other people's imaginations.

It was an act of faith to share the vision—a statement that my belief in God's direction was stronger than my own fears. So I left the security of the known and headed toward my destiny. People's responses were encouraging. "I've never thought of that, but I think it's a real possibility. You should push on that more," they said. I saw their eyes brighten, their passion kick in. I knew the dream was working in them just as it was working in me.

On the other hand, Angel was concerned that I was fading away physically.

"Why don't you eat something?" she said toward the end of the fast. "You've gone long enough and dropped so much weight. Why not end a few days early? You've sacrificed enough."

In truth, the second half of the fast was much more difficult than the first. I was bored by my limited food choices. Each night after getting home from work, I sat in a chair, watched the news, and went to bed early because I was so depleted of energy.

But inwardly I was gaining confidence day by day. For the first time ever in ministry, I felt the wind of the Spirit at my back. The words of Jesus to his disciples came alive for me: "You will receive power when the Holy Spirit has come upon you, and you will be my witnesses" (Acts 1:8). I began to insert my name in the verse and say it out loud. "You, Luke, will receive power when the Holy Spirit has come upon you, and you will be my witness." It was a little gimmicky, but it filled me with confidence to personalize those words and repeat them to myself throughout the day.

Finally, the fast ended and I was brimming with excitement to tell the church what I had experienced. I stood before them and shared the dream God had given me. I focused specifically on the dream to build our new lobby extension debt free. I had learned during my time of fasting that if we continued to pay our regular mortgage payments, we'd be debt free in exactly ten years, the year 2023. God was confirming that I was on the right track! But if we borrowed $8 million to build our new grand lobby, we wouldn't reach the dream of being debt free. We needed a plan, and I believed God had given me one. I told the church, "In thirty days we'll be taking what I'm calling a miracle offering, and we'll apply the money toward this building project and see how God inspires us to get behind this dream." I informed the church that we'd be taking a miracle offering every year until the project was completely funded.

Any leader knows when you set yourself up for a test like that, you want it to go well. Thirty days later the time for the miracle offering came. I had no idea how the church would respond. We had been building facilities for fifteen years straight and had just completed the Prayer Pavilion on the mountain. To ask them to give $8 million toward another building was a real stretch.

After the service that day, Dad and I went out to play golf to get my mind off the offering. I told our business administrator, who counts the offerings every Sunday, to text me the moment she knew how much had come in.

"What do you think, Luke? How much do you guess came in?" Dad asked as we teed off.

"I don't know, Dad," I said, trying to push the thought away. "One hundred thousand? Three hundred thousand?"

I swung at the ball and watched it sail in the blue sky. I turned back to Dad.

"What do you think came in?" I asked.

"Five hundred thousand," he said. Dad always seems to dream bigger than I do!

Just then my phone buzzed. On the screen was a single number: $1.7 million. If I were ever to have a heart attack from surprise, it would have been then.

"What was it?" Dad asked eagerly.

"Do you want to hear?" I said, playing with him.

"Come on, Luke," he said.

"One point seven."

He looked at me in disbelief. Barnetts play a lot of cruel jokes, so I couldn't blame him.

"Are you messing with me?" he said. "One point seven million?"

I showed him the phone.

A praise session began right there on the third hole. Our hearts were so full of gratitude and visions of God's plans that the golf game ended right then. I didn't need a huge offering to confirm that the dream had been from God, but it was an amazing demonstration that the church was behind it all the way.

I was about to discover what it means to lead from a dream.

PART TWO

DREAM-
CENTERED
LIVING

4

The Dream
Begins Again

I took the time to share my journey in the first part of this book because a lot of people are like me—they don't consider themselves born dreamers or visionary leaders but find themselves in circumstances where a God-given dream is an absolute requirement for success. Before my forty-day fast, I had one set of tools. When I arrived at my next task, I saw that, though useful, those tools would not get the job done. As leadership coach Marshall Goldsmith wrote, "What got you here won't get you there."* I needed something more. Much more.

It was a big risk for me to lay everything aside to try to grasp God's dream for me. I was admitting that I didn't know best, that I was actually a weak leader, that my own strength was not enough. But when I humbled myself to that fact, I experienced an infusion of purpose and power unlike anything I had ever known before in my personal life or ministry calling. I believe the same will happen when you pay the price to discover God's dream for you.

In the next few chapters, I'm going to talk about the principles and surprises I discovered about dream-centered living and leadership. These

---

* Marshall Goldsmith, *What Got You Here Won't Get You There* (New York: Hyperion, 2007), 10.

come straight from my own experiences and the observations of others around me. I think they represent the very best practices for a leader or anyone who is ready to pursue a dream-centered life.

Dreams are at the heart of God's plan for each one of us, but they don't come easy. Proverbs 25:2 tells us, "It is the glory of God to conceal things, but the glory of kings is to search things out." God "conceals" our dreams from us to see who is eager and energetic enough to search them out. He's not going to give his best ideas to the lazy. It's like the gold in the hills—it's there, but we have to dig for it. That's why easy solutions are cheap, but everything of lasting value starts with a dream.

Every successful business, every great work of art, every engrossing movie, every innovative product, every inspiring ministry began with a dream that someone paid the price to get. The teachings of Buddha say that all suffering comes from desire, so desire must be eliminated. This is the opposite of what the Bible teaches. It tells us that God gives us desires—dreams—and then fulfills them, not eliminates them. He has very specific dreams for your life. The question is, will you take the time to discover them?

When I talk about dreaming, I'm not talking about optimism, though optimism is good. An optimist was falling from the Empire State Building. As he passed the fourteenth floor, he was heard to say, "So far, so good." Optimism ultimately represents your perspective on a situation, which can be right or wrong. A dream is much more than that. It is a supernatural fact. We can conjure up optimism about any situation, but a dream goes far beyond our personal assessment. It is something true from God's perspective—and his perspective is the one that represents reality.

Be careful before you jump in. A dream is a wild thing. We don't control it at all, though we can cooperate with it. Most dreams take us through twists and turns, ebbs and flows, ups and downs. Some dreams don't kick in until late in life. Colonel Sanders was sixty-five when he started Kentucky Fried Chicken. Miguel de Cervantes was fifty-three when his great novel, *Don Quixote,* was published. My dad was sixty when he started the Los Angeles Dream Center.

But God-sized dreams can be tough going. They lead inevitably to greatness but are seldom easy along the way. They stretch us way beyond our natural abilities. In high school I made the varsity basketball team, probably because the school was so small there wasn't much competition! I was five foot four and soon learned that our coach was a fanatic for stretching. We stretched thirty minutes before and thirty minutes after each practice. We all thought it was a little much at first. At the start of the season I could barely swat the bottom of the net. But due to the daily stretching, at the end of the season I could nick the bottom of the rim! By stretching my body, I had stretched my abilities.

In the same way, a God-sized dream stretches us in ways we don't imagine—and it's both uncomfortable and exhilarating. God-sized dreams build our character. While we are busy working on the dream, God is busy working on us! He builds resilience, persistence, self-control, and much more into who we are, using the dream as his tool.

God-sized dreams also give us much more energy than we had before. They intercept the law of entropy in our lives. They shake off the boredom. So many people sleepwalk through their existence. A famous children's prayer goes, "If I should die before I wake," but many adults need to pray, "Lord, wake me up before I die." They are following the natural path of entropy, which says that without intentional upkeep, everything slowly wastes away on its own—our cars, our homes, our bodies. Dreams interrupt, intercept, and reverse that law. They infuse us with heavenly power for earthly tasks and make us feel fully alive, sometimes for the first time.

Dreams are not easy, but they make us great. Why settle for ease when greatness is possible?

I'm sure my staff got tired of hearing about fasting and dreaming. I was in the middle of the revelation and wanted so badly for everyone around me to experience it as well. With zeal I challenged people to press into God, no matter the cost. Amazingly, our church members and staff caught the vision and caught it strong. People saw that I wasn't trumpeting some idea I had come up with but had apprehended the Lord's plan for all of us. They sensed I had heard from heaven.

Arts Capital of Arizona

Some success happened immediately. As I mentioned, for years our church had used drama in pioneering ways. Dad's illustrated sermons involved a blend of preaching and acting woven together throughout the service. Using that history of innovation as a base of strength, I told our drama director I wanted more. I wanted him to write seven- or eight-minute skits every week to set the stage for the message. I committed to let him know the topic three or four months in advance. That excited him and his team. Before then they didn't have a weekly outlet for their creativity. Now ideas began to flow out of their team at a higher level, and the dramas became an important and popular aspect of church life.

They also responded well to the dream I thought might stretch us too far: having a third production every year, in addition to Easter and Christmas. Imagine my surprise when they said they had already been discussing the possibility in their meetings! They immediately took their plans and began preparing for a summer musical the following year. Strategically, they used our Christmas show, with a cast and crew of four hundred people and an audience of tens of thousands, as a recruiting opportunity.

It worked amazingly well. The truth is, we had no idea if anyone would show up for *Seussical the Musical,* our first presentation. The budget was more than $30,000. I knew it was possible we would take a bath on it, sinking all that money without much return. To our surprise, the show actually brought in revenue. Audience members even began demanding that we charge for tickets to our Christmas show. They wanted their own seats and were willing to pay fifteen to twenty-five dollars to get them. So we began charging, and the shows became even more popular. (We also give away twenty thousand seats over the course of sixteen shows.) We presented *Mary Poppins* the following year, with Mary making her entrance "flying" on a wire. By then our cast and crew were a thousand people strong, and the show not only blessed the community but also brought in revenue to be used for ministry by the church.

It blessed a specific community in Phoenix as well—the LGBT community. We decided that auditions for cast members for the summer show would be open to all participants, Christian or not. If God was giving us a vision to reach the entire state for him, we had to see this as an opportunity to speak into the lives of people who were far from God. From the start, we felt strongly that God would use our excellence and stature in the arts to draw people to him.

We did lose some people at the church because we opened the door to the LGBT community. However, I have always believed that every person matters to God, so every person needs to matter to us. People of all different backgrounds auditioned for the musicals, were given parts, and became valuable members of the team. We had well-thought-out guidelines for participation. Most of the people involved were strong followers of Jesus, so the nature and values of the community were not compromised. Every night the drama director held a mandatory pre-program presentation and kept the gospel and the purpose of the performances before the team. Soon, we began to hear from people who never thought they would consider going to church but who were following Jesus because they had taken a first step toward him by participating in our musicals. We knew God was up to something more than we had imagined.

The arts aspect of the dream from God exploded from the start. Within eighteen months we were selling seven thousand tickets per show and doing two full weekends of Broadway-caliber performances. God provided more leaders and workers who grabbed hold of the vision and ran with it. It was a beautiful resurgence of arts among us in a way only God could have done.

SMALL GROUPS GET BIG

The second surprise for me was in the area of small groups. God had made it very clear to me that fifty thousand people would belong to small groups in our church. That was a staggering number, especially because unlike other churches we didn't have a strong small-groups program. It simply wasn't the culture of our church. People tended to find community in their areas of service rather than in small groups.

God, I have no idea how to even start in this direction, I prayed. *You'll have to lead.*

I had announced the vision, with no idea how to pursue it. One day a staff member came to me.

"Have you heard about a man in our church named Brad Small?" he asked.

I had not, but I soon learned that Brad had come to Phoenix to serve in a large church across town. He previously had been the pastor of a megachurch in Texas whose growth was based on small groups. He was considered a small-groups genius. But he had stepped down from ministry for a season for personal reasons, and the church he belonged to in Phoenix basically disowned him. I didn't know it, but Brad and his wife had started coming to our church right when I became the lead pastor.

They were faithfully attending week after week. Brad was even serving as an usher.

The Lord seemed to be in the timing of Brad's coming, so we went to lunch. By this time he had been out of ministry for three years.

"Brad, would you coach us on how to do small groups?" I asked him. "We know it's part of our future, but we don't know how to do it. I don't even know if you're ready to get back into ministry, but maybe this is God's way of opening new doors for both of us."

As my dad had often found, the miracle was right in the house. Brad became an essential part of our staff and was soon our primary teaching pastor on Wednesday nights. Because of him and the Lord's blessing on his task, our Wednesday services grew like crazy. And he put rocket fuel in our small-groups plan and made it soar. We stood in awe and knew it was a sign of God's provision that he had sent Brad at just the right time.

DEBT-FREE CAMPUS

After the first miracle offering of $1.7 million came in, the architects started drawing up plans for our new grand lobby, but I had to wonder if the money would continue to come in to support the effort. We took a second miracle offering the following year, and the total was even higher: $1.9 million. That's a phenomenal amount of money to come in at any church on a single weekend. I never dreamed I would see such large offerings in my lifetime as a pastor. A third miracle offering the year after that brought $1.7 million more, and we knew God was strongly affirming our work.

The following October we took our fourth miracle offering. At 7:00 that Sunday night, I was at home waiting for the church's business manager to text me with the amount. As the hours dragged on, I told Angel, "My business manager is afraid to even tell me the number. The people must be so worn out. It must be so low that she doesn't want to text me."

It wasn't long before the text arrived, and the number staggered me: $2.5 million. I didn't even know what to think, but Angel and I knew we were seeing the hand of God move in an amazing way. The only place open that time of night on Sunday was Denny's, so we drove there to celebrate a $2.5 million offering.

When I told my dad the size of the offering, the phone went quiet. Then he said, "You're lying to me. This does not happen." For the first time in my memory, Dad was speechless. After I convinced him I was telling the truth, he rejoiced with us and was happier than anyone.

People were responding to the dream in a massive way and putting their pocketbooks behind it. Nobody was dragging their heels or asking, "Why are we doing this?" Rather, they were saying, "What do we need to do to make this happen?" We were able to build the new grand lobby long before our hoped-for deadline without incurring any debt.

As a leader, I had never experienced anything like it. In a matter of months, I went from despair and crippling self-doubt to tremendous, peaceful confidence that God was behind us. He was honoring the plans because the people were listening to his dream. For the first time in my ministry career, I knew we were going from glory to glory.

Dreamless living is a dim, colorless existence. I spent far too many years there. The Bible assures us that without a vision, people simply perish (see Proverbs 29:18, KJV). The word for *perish* in biblical Hebrew comes from the word meaning "out of control." That described my ministry before receiving God's dream. I felt out of control in the sense that I felt at the mercy of the forces around me. At best I could steady and guide the ship somewhat, but the effort was great and the results were less than I wanted. Dreamless living feels powerless in so many ways. These feelings told me things weren't working right, that I was perishing in ministry.

Without a dream, people feel like pawns in the grand scheme of things because they feel unable to navigate toward a good future. To not have a dream is a form of blindness and desperation. As Helen Keller said, "The only thing worse than being blind is having sight and no vision." That was me, and maybe it has been you at some point. The truth is most people go through life without a God-given dream. They drift along feeling out of control. When you can't see how your business or marriage or life will improve and you struggle to get excited about anything, you have lost your vision. Dreamlessness saps you of energy. Stress goes up; emotional and physical health go down.

Our entire experience of life is tied to having a God-given dream.

Yes!

DREAMING THROUGH FALSE STARTS

The one area of God's dream for us that didn't move ahead was the vision for a multisite campus. Ironically, that's the one I tried hardest to make happen—and learned some hard lessons.

When I shared the multisite vision, a very good member of the church approached me and said he had a relative who was involved in church planting at a large church in another state and had been a leader in this area for years.

"I would be willing to pay his salary if you would bring him on staff," this man told me. It seemed like an open door, and we knew we needed leadership to make multisite happen. So we interviewed the man, brought him on staff, and set aside a budget for him to work with.

Within a short time, the man was clashing with our culture and plans. Right away he felt dissatisfied because we weren't taking his advice and buying a building or renting a storefront in which to start other church sites. He wanted it to happen yesterday, but I told him that's not how we operate. We build relationships, put the antenna up, and look for God to bring opportunities that make sense in his time. This was especially the case because, unlike some other churches' budgets, much of our budget was going toward major outreaches. The money other churches might spend on planting churches, we were spending on huge ministries to feed the poor and care for the needy.

I learned tough but insightful lessons during this part of our journey:

- Some people are accustomed to walking by sight, not by faith. They won't believe it unless they see it, and they think you're moving ahead only if your accomplishments are tangible. That tension grew and grew as we defined *success* differently.

- The biggest disagreements will be about culture. Yes, we were at odds over how to spend the money set aside for multisite projects, but the bigger issue was attitude. Speaking from my own experience, I have found the greatest unity and loyalty comes from raising people up from within. The culture is ingrained in them. They chose to belong before they were ever paid. Those who come from outside have a learning curve, and they may struggle to become a son or daughter of the ministry. Learning to shape and maintain the proper culture is a critical lesson for leaders as they hire people.

- Criticism doesn't have boundaries. What I mean is, when people are willing to criticize one aspect of an organization, they will be critical of other things too.

- It's best to hire slow and fire fast. If it's not working with an employee, it's not working. You don't want to prolong it. The best path is to take a long time to make sure it is the right fit from the get-go.

Two years after God gave me the vision, we hadn't advanced one bit on having multisite campuses across the state. That's when I started doubting that aspect of the dream. *Maybe I got my signals crossed when I thought I heard this,* I thought. *Maybe that was a man-made dream. All the other four are going strong, even though I've poured more energy into this one than all the others combined. God, I'm done pushing this one. If that part of the dream was from you, you'll have to do it. I've done everything I can.*

I left it there.

Somewhere deep inside I sensed that maybe we weren't ready to go multisite yet, and one reason may have been that we were still rebuilding our infrastructure after a painful parting with a ministry that had grown up at our church and then imploded.

LETTING OLD DREAMS DIE

Rewind a couple of years to when I returned to Phoenix after serving in California. At that time a ministry aimed at college-age students, which had been birthed and grown nationwide from Phoenix First, was running all the children's and youth ministries at the church. It had a budget of $700,000 a year, which is huge, and though it provided valuable service to the church for many years, eventually there were tensions that could no longer be ignored.

For various reasons, the staff at this ministry and the church board were at odds. Having recently come on staff at the church, I asked my dad if I could go speak to that ministry's leaders and try a rapprochement.

"I think I can resolve this relationship and get us through," I said hopefully.

Dad allowed it, and my meeting with the team seemed to go very well. A number of people cried and told me, "No one has reached out to us like this." I left believing it was a good meeting, though one of the leaders had ended it by asking for more funding, which caught me sideways.

Within weeks we heard something we almost couldn't believe: the leader of this ministry, along with many other leaders, was planning to launch a church just a few miles from our campus, which would have split our church apart. Over the years my dad had encouraged many of the families in our church to open their homes and provide a residence for the students of this program. Starting a church a few miles away would have forced many families to choose between our church and the new one.

That was the last straw for Dad. He hates firing people, but he called the leader in. That was the beginning of the end. A few weeks later the leader and others moved en masse to another state to start a church there.

This experience taught me several lessons I have held on to:

- Churches often provide a covering for other ministries to grow. When a ministry leaves that umbrella of safety, support, and partnership, things can deteriorate.

- For any ministry to make it in a season of change, the leaders must humble themselves in the sight of the Lord and be willing to adjust. If they don't follow new directions, they become irrelevant.

- Perhaps most important, I realized that before new dreams can take off, old dreams have to die. Some old dreams simply slow down or shift direction. Others come to the end of their cycle, and it's appropriate to let them go. Soon we realized that God had new plans for us that required our budget and energy to go in new directions. While losing that ministry and those people felt confusing and devastating, it freed up resources that helped us build new things. It also caused us to hire new, young leaders in key ministries, which strengthened our organization in places we were weak before. That prepared us for a season of breakthrough.

Looking back, I was grateful that this battle was fought early on rather than during the time God was releasing our dream. God was preparing a way for us to pursue a new vision.

Mom's Pantry

God also prepared the way by giving us glimpses of what big dreams looked like even before I went into that season of oppression and the forty-day fast. One of those glimpses began in my wife's heart and made me hungry for God's dream. Angel told me one day, "We really need a food distribution center near the church. God has really laid it on my heart. I'm going to start looking at buildings."

Honestly, I didn't take her seriously. "Go ahead, but we don't have money to do it right now," I said, dismissing the idea.

Angel kept praying and believing for a building that we could use as a food pantry near our church. One day she told me, "You know, there's a building across the street, a big industrial space of twelve thousand square feet, for sale for $400,000. It probably needs work, but it would be perfect for a food pantry."

Once again I didn't give the idea much serious thought, but whenever we drove by the warehouse, Angel held her hand out as we passed and prayed, "I believe that building will belong to us for the purpose of having a food bank for poor people."

She took it one step further and got contractors to meet her at the industrial building to talk about renovations. They worked out what it would cost to install heating, ventilation, and air-conditioning, plus plumbing and more—about $400,000, which meant $800,000 to purchase and upgrade. Angel didn't have any money, but she kept dreaming. She was living out the truth that you can welcome your dream before you have any evidence of it.

That went on for months. "In Jesus's name, give us that building," Angel prayed every time we drove by. Of course, I had done this and seen my parents and siblings do this many times—walking in something by faith before it became real. When you see enough wins, you believe that God will really respond to your faith. I started to admire Angel for standing boldly for this dream. It also provoked me. Because I was not a natural dreamer, I began to feel the power of Angel's dream and got a little jealous! With no outward sign of hope and a husband who was unenthusiastic, she possessed enough faith to keep believing in her dream. I was about to see what such faith could do.

One day we were having lunch with friends who had just sold their aerospace aluminum business.

"We actually didn't want to sell the business," they told us. "Things were going well, but these buyers flew out to our ranch, and we threw out a number that was so astronomical we knew they wouldn't take it. They walked around for a while, came back, and said, 'We'll do it.' So we tested it again by saying, 'We need another $800,000 for a project the Lord has for us.' They went out, talked again, and agreed."

I could see Angel's eyes sparkling. Then the couple said the unthinkable: "So we have $800,000 to use for ministry, and we would like to do something particularly in the area of feeding people. Do you have any ideas or projects you're working on?"

"As a matter of fact," Angel said and began spelling out her vision for a food pantry near the church.

The next day the couple was at the building with her. They were convinced it was God's plan for their money. Before I knew it, they had bought the building and installed new everything—equipment, racks, walk-in freezers, and more to the tune of $800,000.

Just like that, Mom's Pantry was born. All because Angel listened to the dream God put in her heart. It's interesting that Angel didn't fight God's dream; she just received it by faith and said, "Thank you, Lord, for that building," every time we drove by.

Our drama team later decided that part of the proceeds from their shows would go to support Mom's Pantry. They began raising tens of thousands of dollars for Mom's Pantry and another ministry of ours that bloomed in downtown Phoenix.

DREAM ROOMS

Years earlier our church had started a Dream Center in a former Embassy Suites hotel in downtown Phoenix that we had bought for just under $5 million. For four years, the thing was a headache—Dad hadn't found the right leader for it, and he pledged more than once to shut it down because it wasn't having much of an impact.

Then Brian Steele, one of the volunteers at the Phoenix Dream Center, came onto our radar. He was a self-starter and highly motivated for that kind of ministry. We hired him, and Brian revolutionized the place. It went from being a headache to being a blessing for our city and our church. We loved hearing about the good things happening there.

One day a newspaper ran an article about Phoenix being a hub of human sex trafficking because of its proximity to the border with Mexico. Our church leadership was distressed by that, so with Dad and Brian leading us, we decided to make ten rooms at the Phoenix Dream Center into places where victims of sex trafficking could live while they rebuilt their lives. A home builder in our church had relationships with interior designers and builders all over Scottsdale. He heard about the plan and said, "What if we approached these high-end designers to see if they will adopt a room?" The rooms needed to be renovated so they didn't feel like any of the hotel rooms where the sex trafficking victims had been enslaved before. We needed the rooms to feel like heaven, to really show the women how special and honored they were now.

The home builder shared the idea in his community of builders and designers, and there was a lot of interest in helping. Then a big Scottsdale magazine decided to hold a contest to see who could renovate a room at the Dream Center in the most creative and awesome way. More interior designers called and wanted to participate. They spent anywhere from $50,000 to $100,000 per room, even flying in wood from old barns in Italy for the floors and walls. These rooms ended up looking much better than any of our homes, and the contest raised a bunch of publicity about helping these women. It was a huge win for everyone.

We ended up renovating eight more rooms, specifically for girls who had gotten pregnant and were no longer useful to their pimps in their sordid occupation. When the police conduct a sting and bust the pimps, they often call us so we can be there to offer our rooms as a place for the women to stay. From the start there was a waiting list for these beautiful rooms. Today we have the third largest human sex trafficking ministry in America and have helped rescue more than three hundred young women since 2012.

Mom's Pantry and the Dream Rooms showed Angel and me something we hadn't seen: big dreams in action. When I went into my defining time with God, those two projects were very much in my mind, undergirding my confidence that there was even more for our church to accomplish. Not only did God clear the way by pruning old, uncooperative ministries, but he gave us real-life visions of what he could do if we let our imaginations soar with him.

Let me summarize those early lessons:

- God-sized dreams are more than optimism. They are God's vision for us. That means they feel big, wild, and out of our control. They stretch us in ways we may not expect, but they also make us great.

- God provides for his dreams in unexpected ways. We discovered our amazing small-groups leader right in our midst. You will have many such surprises as you lead and live from a dream.

- God does financial miracles to support the vision and encourage the people. This doesn't mean it's always easy financially or that you always feel you have the money needed for the task. But when a dream comes from God, he pays the bills.

- Some dreams happen after a few false starts. This may be a way our faith is tested, or it might just be the learning process we all have to go through. The question is, will you stick with the dream even when it seems like you've hit a dead end? When you do, it will eventually get traction.

- Old dreams must die to make way for new dreams.

- The new dreams are always better!

5

Dream Busters

The biggest enemies of a God-given dream are what I call dream busters. These are the people around you who don't see or appreciate the dream the way you do. Kind of like the way I responded to Angel's dream.

I have learned how to handle dream busters because they are an occupational hazard for any dream-centered leader. The principles in this chapter are not just slogans for me. I've road tested each of them, sometimes at a greater cost than I would have liked. Let's dive in and see how to handle some of the dream busters you will probably encounter.

EVERYONE STARTS WITH A DREAM

Dream busters don't start as dream busters. Everyone has a dream from a young age, but most people lose it somewhere along the way. That's the sad truth about life. When people let go of their dreams, they don't want you to have a hold on yours either. Seeing someone walking in their destiny makes them feel bad. Some will ignore your dream, and some will actually try to harm it.

I heard a story about a young boy whose teacher asked the class to write descriptions of their dreams. The boy wrote about his dream of owning a big horse ranch with a hundred horses and people to ride them. The teacher graded the paper and handed it back with a big F.

"Your dream is out of touch with reality," she said. "You don't want to disappoint yourself. I'll let you redo it and give you another grade."

The boy took the paper and thought for a moment. After a while he handed it back to the teacher with no changes.

"You keep the F," he told her. "I'll keep my dream."

That boy's dream came true. When he grew up he did own a horse ranch. That teacher later apologized for what she did. "When I was a teacher, I stole a lot of kids' dreams," she said. "Fortunately, you had enough gumption to hold on to yours."

My dad was the opposite of that teacher. He taught us to pull for underdogs, to go out of our way to raise people to a new level—to empower dreams. I watched Dad find disenfranchised people nobody else had interest in. He almost rubbed it in the noses of elite people who felt above that kind of ministry. Dad knew better. He told us, "If you build a church with people nobody wants, God will give you people that everybody wants." That was true. We had many multimillionaires and celebrities at our churches because they wanted to belong to a place that empowered people's dreams. They could see the benefit that their giving and support was having on the poor.

Dad often took Matthew and me to inner-city parks on weeknights to play hoops with guys there. He wanted us to play with people who outmatched us, and he always said the same thing no matter how fierce the other team looked: "Come on, we can take them." When choosing teams he intentionally chose underdogs, the guys nobody wanted. Somehow he always made us believe we could win, even with an inferior squad. I'm not bragging when I say that we won most of those games. We had something greater than physical ability: we had the belief in a dream that was outrageous enough to seem possible. No dream buster could touch us.

The power of belief can propel us to surprising successes. When I was twenty years old, Matthew and I put together a basketball tournament at our church and invited anyone to participate. We got the idea from college Christmas Classics and held the tournament in December. Phoenix First had just built a new gym with a beautiful weight room, and I was serving as athletic coordinator. Fifteen teams from all over the city, mostly larger churches, signed up.

Our team made it to the finals to play against another team. Thankfully, Matthew and I didn't know that the opposing team had wiped out everyone by thirty or more points while our team had eked out our victories. The tournament was double elimination, and we had one loss. They were undefeated, meaning that to win the big prize, we had to beat them twice in a row.

Game time rolled around. The gymnasium was packed. As we took to the court, nobody on our team knew why their team was so strong: they had recruited their players from a local college team that had just won a national championship at their level of play. We were basically playing national champions in different uniforms.

It was heated competition from the first jump ball. I felt like the game never slowed down, and by the last minute, we were down by just one point. The place was going crazy. You could smell the sweat and feel the heat. With five seconds to go, I drove in for a layup. Their huge forward blocked my shot, but it bounced back into my hands and I laid it in. Time ran out and we won. We were exultant. Matthew and I ran over to my dad to celebrate with him.

"Do you realize what you've done?" Dad said. "That's not just any team. Those guys just won the national championship in their college league!"

It was an incredible moment for us, but we still had one game to play. You might guess what happened next. Before that first game, when we didn't know who the other team was, we brimmed with confidence. But now intimidation spread like a disease. *We can't compete with those guys,* we thought. *They just won a national championship.*

Sure enough, in the second game they smoked us. We got second place.

Believing in our dream helped us win a great victory. Then dream-busting fear stole our confidence, and we collapsed. I learned a huge lesson about maintaining high expectations no matter the odds. It's probably what kept me in the saddle in difficult assignments later. The power of expectation, of holding on to a dream, elevates your level of stamina and strength. It brings out the dreams and faith in those around you too. I think of the shepherd boy David, who single-handedly defeated the giant. His great expectation and subsequent victory caused the soldiers in Israel's army to suddenly have enough courage to chase down and defeat their enemies—enemies who had intimidated them for months. One man's expectations raised the level of an entire army.

If that's not leadership, I don't know what is.

High expectations and big dreams probably explain why nearly all the leaders at our church were raised up here, not imported from elsewhere. First, we believed in them enough to empower them. Second, nobody had a chance to lower their expectations. I don't think other leaders intend to spread fear and doubt. They may sound sensible and wise. But if you listen to dream-busting words and ideas, they keep you from launching into your best future.

Here are the main facts and warnings about dream busters, as I see them.

Dream Busters Teach Us Who We Really Fear

If you are going to be a dream-centered person, you're going to have to decide who you fear—God or people. For much of my early ministry, I was a people pleaser. I feared disapproval, so I sometimes made decisions based on that fear. That was poor leadership. This type of leadership harmed the places I was serving, it dimmed the dream, and it put me in a trap. There is no greater trap than fear. It is the opposite of a faith-filled dream.

By the time I came back to Phoenix, I had mostly overcome the habit of making people-pleasing decisions. I had learned to bite the bullet, accept potential rejection, and choose the best decision anyway.

Recently, at a community fund-raiser, a ministry colleague and I found ourselves sitting at a table with ten guys I didn't know. The subject of churches came up, and one guy became particularly vocal about his disgust with a certain local church.

"That place has so much traffic during the Christmas season that it shuts down the neighborhood. It's chaotic," he said. "Someone told me that the church is cultish. They have their own community, their own coffee shop, their own workout facility and gymnasium. I heard the leader is cultish too. People gather just to hear him talk about stuff. He's kind of a cult leader."

My ministry colleague ventured to ask, "Where is this church located?"

The man answered with the name of our street. Instead of chiming in, I just sat and listened. I was interested in what else he would blame us for. He ranted a few more minutes, making wildly unfair judgments about our church based on hearsay. At that point we had to leave to keep our schedule elsewhere, so I told the man in parting, "You might want to attend that church sometime so you can form an accurate opinion."

"Not gonna happen," he said instantly. "I'm not drinking the Kool-Aid."

By then my friend couldn't contain himself. He laughed and said, "Luke is the pastor of that church."

This guy didn't miss a beat. He put his hand out and said, "Nice to meet you, Mr. David Koresh." He was referring to the cult leader of the Branch Davidians in Waco, Texas. In 1993 Koresh led his followers in a standoff with federal agents, which ended when the compound burned down.

In an earlier season of my life, that conversation would have caused me a lot of angst. I might have gone back and wondered how we could improve our reputation in the community. I might have made practical decisions about parking and performances based on that one man's criticism. But I had learned not to fear the disapproval of others.

You have the choice: you can live to please God or to please people. Which will it be? The answer will tell you a lot about where you are in life. Any time you fear someone more than God, you allow that person to disable you. Proverbs 29:25 calls fear of people a snare. A snare holds you and keeps you from going anywhere or doing anything. Fear is the greatest disabling condition on the planet, and millions of people have it. They live with disabled emotions, disabled dreams. They constantly ask, "What would my boyfriend think if I went all out for my God-given dream? What would my family think? What would my friends think?"

The book of Proverbs also assures us that trusting in God protects us from death (see 14:27). Here's one of the greatest secrets I have learned: It's no use caring what other people think about you because nobody's really thinking about you. People are so self-centered that they are always thinking of themselves and how they are perceived. We would fear people's opinions a whole lot less if we knew how infrequently they thought of us.

You Have Been a Dream Buster More Often Than You Think

Some guy told my dad, "You're going to start a work in Los Angeles? Really? A Dream Center? What's that? That'll never work. You're wasting your time flying out there so much."

Who was that horrible person? Ahem. That was me.

I recognize dream busters because I have been one so many times—and so have you. I already told the story of Angel's dream to start Mom's Pantry and my pathetic initial response. Unfortunately, I've responded that way more times than I can count.

One time my father-in-law, who loved the sea, bought an old sailboat. This thing had been so badly abused and neglected by its owner that it seemed hopeless. The wood was rotting, parts were missing, and all sorts of things were broken and looked irreparable. I was one of the several voices in our family who gently mocked him for buying it. "That thing belongs in a junkyard," we said. "You'll be paying someone to haul it away next summer."

But he patiently worked on that boat over the winter. He sanded the wood, replaced broken parts, and lacquered and painted it. By the time we visited him again the next summer, I was amazed. The boat looked better than new. It had a new mast, a new foresail, new brass parts, and revitalized wood and interior—it was just plain awesome. I had to eat my words, and I realized I had been a dream buster.

Maybe you'll recognize yourself in this joke, which unfortunately describes a lot of people: A woman took her husband to the doctor for a checkup, then came back later to pick him up. The receptionist said, "Ma'am, your husband is in critical condition."

"What?" The woman asked. "When I dropped him off, he was fine."

"He's in very critical condition," the receptionist said again. "He's critical of the doctors, critical of the nurses, critical of me, critical of the equipment, critical of the waiting room . . ."

Does that describe you? Are you going around busting people's dreams? Maybe you don't think so, but spend some time listening to your own words. You may be surprised.

One more example and then I'll stop picking on myself. My dad used to say to the congregation, "I believe God is going to bless some of your businesses. Your motives are pure. You want to bless your family and the work of God's kingdom. I believe someone here is going to give a million dollars to this church someday."

I was a little kid at the time and thought, *You're crazy, Dad. No one's going to give a million dollars.* I didn't realize there were people in the congregation at that time who wanted to give that much and were financially able to do it. I'm here to tell you that on eighteen different occasions someone gave a million dollars to the church for God's work. Dad was right.

Now Dad stands before people and says, "I believe someone here is going to give a billion dollars to God's work someday." I was actually embarrassed for him the first time he said it because it seemed so preposterous. But I had to look back on his track record! Now I think God will grant him that dream. There are certainly business people in our church who want to build Dream Centers all across the earth. I hear them talk about trying to be successful so they can fulfill the dream of giving a billion dollars for the work of God. They are actually trying to do it! Maybe we all need to get bolder about asking.

Each of us can point to examples of busting someone's dream. I squirm to think about it, but it's an automatic reaction for some of us, and we must train ourselves out of it. The good news is that people can change. Back when Dad was starting the Dream Center in LA and the whole concept was new, everyone was telling him not to go. One man, a close friend of Dad's, said, "You don't need to go to LA, Tommy. It's just going to wear you out and take away from the work here in Phoenix. I'm concerned about you."

Within two years that very man and his son gave $2 million to save the Dream Center from being closed down because of needed structural upgrades. He went from being a dream buster to a dream lifter. We can all do the same.

Your Family and Closest Friends Will Often Be Your Most Challenging Dream Busters

When I fasted and got the dream of God for our church, not everyone was as excited as I was. Nobody came right out and challenged me, but a few leaders and close associates were obviously unenthusiastic. Sometimes they patted me on the back and said things like, "I'm glad you have something you're excited about."

That hurt my feelings more than a direct challenge! How could they not be as excited about this God-given dream as I was? Couldn't they see the future of our church?

I came to believe that sometimes God allows dream busters to be our own close friends and family for a season. He does it to test us. When I first became senior pastor at Phoenix First, I often sought wise counsel from older mentors I trusted. Their wisdom had kept me on track for many years. But as I grew as a leader, I began to feel that often their voices conflicted with my dream.

For example, when I laid out the idea for a multisite church, one mentor in particular tried to discourage me out of genuine concern for me.

"Do you really want to do this?" he asked. "Phoenix First is a huge campus with so many ministries impacting so many people. If you try to have other campuses, it means so many more headaches. It might steal your overall impact."

I had to wrestle with that, especially when the multisite idea seemed dead in the water. I also respected this man a great deal. Then one day it dawned on me: God had given the vision to me, not to my mentor. It didn't make this man my enemy, but it tested my faith in the dream. He was not called to lead the church toward this dream in this season. He hadn't prayed and fasted about it. He hadn't seen the vision so strongly in his mind's eye. I had. It was ultimately my responsibility.

So I chose to follow God's leading against the advice of people I greatly respected and let the chips fall where they may. I did it very respectfully, and I didn't stop seeking their advice. I just had to learn to distinguish between what they said and what God said. In that way, having dream busters so close sharpened me spiritually.

When the dream in your heart is stronger than even the voices of those you trust most, that's when you know it's from God. When the vision captivates you more than anyone's respect or approval, you know you've discovered your life purpose.

One of the best dream stories you will ever encounter is not on the Internet or television; it's the story of Joseph found in the first book of the Bible. Joseph was kind of a daddy's boy. It was obvious to his brothers that he was Daddy's favorite, and his brothers resented him for it. One night while Joseph was sleeping, God dropped a dream in his heart. Joseph dreamed of one day being a great leader. This dream in the night began to stir his heart during the day, and he told his brothers about it. What was their response? Genesis 37:5 tells us, "They hated him even more."

You have probably seen in your own life that natural negative reaction people have when you share your dream. There will always be haters. There will always be people who do not believe in your dream. They'll be negative and cynical about it, and if you let them, they will rip the dream right out of your heart. That is why you have to hold on to your dream. Your dream is too important to God, to you, and to the world to let them rip it from you.

Joseph experienced this to an extreme. His brothers thought of killing him. Instead, they threw him into a pit and then decided to sell him to Egyptian slave traders. So much for the dream! Joseph served as a slave in Egypt and then was unfairly sent to prison, where he spent years of his life. Imagine how ridiculous his dream must have seemed to him during that time. He didn't know yet that leaders are refined in hard circumstances and tough, out-of-the-way places.

We can learn a few lessons from the way Joseph responded.

Keep Your Eyes on the God Who Is for You

The more you focus on the dream busters, the bigger they seem. But when you set your sights on the Dream Giver, nobody can tear that dream away.

Keep Your Eyes on the Dreams in Front of You

Jesus did that when heading to the place of crucifixion. The Bible says he looked beyond that pain to the joy he would have later. Each of us can do that. For example, I make a habit of posting my dreams where I can see them—on a bathroom mirror or the dashboard of the car. We need to remind ourselves of our dreams and reconnect with their energy and excitement, even when their fulfillment seems far away.

Keep Your Eyes on the Dream Team Around You

In other words, build a team of people who are positive and encouraging, even when they disagree with you. Surround yourself with those who see the best in you, and you in them.

When my dream was new and uncertain and I became discouraged at times, I learned the value of having even one person stand with me. One time I began to wonder if it was worth it to focus on big things for God. At that moment I got a text from a friend named Keith. He wrote, "Father, I ask that you bless Luke and make the dream you are dreaming through him come true."

My spirit literally leapt inside me when I read those words. The next week he sent another text: "Praying for you, Luke, that like Caleb, because you have a different spirit, God is going to use you to conquer mountains and giants for the kingdom of God." Those two little messages caused my faith to soar, and I held on to the dream with a stronger grip.

That's what a dream team will do for you. Get around people who will dream big. De-emphasize those relationships that are holding you back.

DREAMS GUARANTEE CONFLICT

By its very nature, your dream is going to offend someone. Even if you are feeding the poor, at some point your dream will come into conflict with someone or with the culture around you. As I follow my dream to do the work I am doing in Arizona, I run into conflict frequently. People don't like my views on social matters, my goal for our organization, or the way I'm doing things. That's just life. Not everyone is going to like every aspect of your dream. In fact, some will hate it, no matter what it is.

I'm not proud of this, but when I was in high school, my friends and I totally froze a kid out of our social circle because he irritated us. He was always setting the curve. We weren't nearly as diligent in our studies. We called him a dweeb and said, "Chill out! Watch more TV at night. Skip a book report now and then." He wasn't trying to irritate us. He was trying to be the best student he could be, but he was an irritant to us. We felt exposed.

Did we study harder and try to excel more? No, we treated him badly. That's exactly what people will try to do to you sometimes. Usually it's because your pursuit of your dream exposes the fact that they are not pursuing a dream. They want you to drift the way they do. It makes them feel better.

This happens all the time in the marketplace. Hopeful, dream-centered people try to do their best, working as effectively and efficiently as they can and avoiding the office politics. Those people automatically become irritants. Proverbs 29:10 says the wicked seek to destroy the life of the upright. Why? Because they are upright! That's all the reason some people need. Pretty soon someone unloads on them: "Will you get off your high horse? Stop thinking you're better than the rest of us. You people are all alike—self-righteous hypocrites."

Okay . . . Where did that come from? It came from your dream, which is a natural irritant.

Settle it now: taking a stand for your dream will cost you some friends. It may even cost you more than that.

I remember talking to a woman who had a very good marriage until she came to Christ. Partying was a big part of her and her husband's lives. When she became a Christian, she didn't lose her love for her husband, but she no longer wanted to be in rooms full of drunk people. God was changing her heart. The marriage breaker was her decision to stop watching pornography with her husband. He began to say evil things against her. But her choice was clear: she wasn't going back to the dream-killing stuff of her past.

DREAM BUSTER FOR JOE

One of the guys I admire for not giving in to dream busters is Joe Martinez. I met Joe when I was serving in California. He had just graduated from a training program in Phoenix, was about to get married, and wanted to be in ministry. Everyone knew he was a man of great integrity, and I liked him a lot. I asked Joe to be part of our team as youth pastor at our church in California. He was excited to join us.

I had just taken the post as senior pastor a few months earlier, and it was a difficult season of transition. I wasn't feeling strong as a leader and was still trying to appease people when I should have stood by my principles. Some parents complained about the direction of the youth group, and in my inexperience I panicked. I called Joe in and said, "I've got to make a change in the youth program. I've got so many parents complaining. I can't afford to keep you on full time." There really weren't that many, but the ones who were complaining were problem people, and I wanted to try to make them happy. Bad idea.

Joe's response was amazing. "I feel called here," he said. "I'll work for free. I didn't come for the salary. I came because this is part of my dream."

Stunned, I offered to pay him half his previous salary to take another position. He cheerfully stayed on, shifted duties, and raised up a very strong young-adults program in the church. He became one of the top three decision makers in that church. Joe was a tremendous example to me even though he was below me on the organizational chart. He wasn't a hireling—he was a man who knew his God-given dream and calling.

One day after I had returned to Phoenix, Joe called.

"I feel like God is calling me to work with you in Phoenix," he said.

I told him, "Please don't move here if you're looking for a job. I don't have any openings, and I can't create something for you right now. If anything opens up, you're the first one I'll call."

Joe said again, "That's fine, but I really feel God is calling us to Phoenix. I'm not expecting a job, but I want to come and serve for free in the ministry."

With his church's blessing, Joe moved to Phoenix with his family. There was no ministry opportunity, and he took no ministry job. At that time, Mom's Pantry was just getting off the ground, and we were already serving nine thousand hot meals a week at the Dream Center.

"We need a real general who can lead our food ministries," I told

Angel one day. She mentioned the need for a leader to the couple who had bought and renovated the building for Mom's Pantry. Joe's name came up, and it turns out this couple knew Joe and his wife!

"We'll pay their salary if you bring them on," this couple said, and so we did. Joe studied the great food-distribution ministries in the country, learned their processes, and has made a significant impact in our community and church. Today, he is the executive pastor of our media and operations, oversees worship and the drama teams, and also continues to oversee Mom's Pantry.

Joe got promoted because he didn't let his dreams get busted, even by knuckleheads like me.

Dreams Birthed in Tragedy

Sometimes dreams are born in the worst possible circumstances.

When Angel and I were serving in California, we decided to have a staff getaway at Lake Mead. An acquaintance's friends owned the company that rented houseboats there and asked if our church staff would like to spend a week on the lake as a free gift. We had been working hard and in crisis circumstances for six months without a break, so I thought it was a great idea. We set the date for the week after Mother's Day.

Our children's pastor, Jeff, and his wife, Beverly, along with their son Derrick and one of our church interns, Paul, arrived at the lake a few hours early to pick up the houseboat, stock it with supplies, and drive both it and the ski boat fifteen miles across the lake to pick up the rest of our staff members on the other side. Jeff and Bev planned to drive the houseboat, while Derrick and Paul would man the ski boat. When they arrived, storm advisories were in effect, but the weather didn't seem bad enough to require a change in plans.

None of our staff members were expert boaters, and when they got on the lake, the wind really picked up. Five-foot waves pounded the houseboat and rushed over the deck. Jeff and Bev began to wonder how Derrick and Paul were faring in the ski boat.

The answer was not well. Ski boats have flat bottoms so they don't create wakes. In choppy waters, flat bottoms are not ideal. It was a good thing Derrick and Paul had life jackets because a wave came over the top, knocked them both into the water, and capsized the boat, leaving it floating vertically with only the nose barely sticking out of the water. They clung to the front of the boat waiting for help. At one point they saw a houseboat go by a hundred yards away, but the people on the houseboat couldn't see them because of the waves.

"I'll swim over, flag them down, and tell them to come back," Derrick said. Within just a few strokes he was out of sight. That was the last Paul saw of Derrick. The waves eventually carried the boat to an island where Paul spent the night in the open. Jeff and Bev's houseboat had been shoved onto the rocks, and they were immobilized until morning.

The next day the lake had calmed down, and we were unloading our Jet Skis to go find Derrick and Paul when the police arrived. They had found Derrick's body washed up on shore. Paul was then found by a fisherman who brought him to the marina.

The horror and grief on Jeff's and Bev's faces when they learned of Derrick's death was the most awful thing I had ever seen. Here I was trying to reward our staff for working so hard, and their son had lost his life. It was one of the greatest heartbreaks that Angel and I have ever experienced.

But God had more to the story. Jeff and Bev returned home and four months later found a piece of paper written by Derrick at a leadership conference at Phoenix First Assembly. On it he had written that his life goal was to create the best sidewalk Sunday school in the West "by any means." Something clicked in Jeff and Bev. They took that dream upon themselves and created such a ministry. Derrick loved fire trucks, so a local fire station donated a fire truck in his name, and Jeff and Bev started Firehouse Kidz. They go into neighborhoods, construct a small stage in front of the fire truck, and tell kids about Jesus Christ using games, fun, and fire hoses blasting water into the air. It's a great thing.

In a way none of us could conceive at the time, tragedy birthed a dream. If you have been through something terrible, or even just something difficult, pay attention to the potential in that circumstance. As tragic as it might be, it may hold the seeds of your dream the way it did for Jeff and Bev.

Let's recap the main points of this chapter:

- Everyone starts with a dream. Each person on planet Earth is born with a God-sized idea of what he or she wants to do and who he or she wants to be. There's no such thing as a dreamless human being.

- Dream busters oppose or minimize people's dreams. They simply don't believe in a God big enough to make dreams come true.

- Dream busters are useful in one way: they challenge us by revealing who we really want to please—God or people. We can't always please both.

- Sadly, each of us has probably been a dream buster to someone at some point. That doesn't make it right, so we must get in the habit of listening to our own words and making a conscious choice to encourage people's dreams.

- The hardest dream busters to overcome are our closest friends and family! I believe God lets it be this way so we choose to stick with our dream. We must discover that the dream in our heart is stronger than the voice of anyone around us.
- Sometimes dreams are born in very difficult circumstances. If you're walking through a tough valley, keep your eyes and heart open for what God wants to do with it.

6

Dream Lifters

For those who think dream-centered living is all pie in the sky, I want to show you how intensely practical it is. I have found my administrative and organizational abilities far more essential in service of a dream than at any other time. God expects us to manage and administer our dreams effectively. I call these habits dream lifters, and they are common to all the dreamers I know. Let's look at some of the most important dream lifters as you launch into the dream-centered life.

DREAMERS MAKE SCHEDULES AND GUARD THEIR CALENDARS

The thoughtful, prayerful crafting of a personal schedule can be one of the holiest endeavors we put our hands to. When we create our calendar, we write the script of who we will become in five, ten, and twenty years. Far more than money or talent, time is every person's most valuable asset. Dreamers must see time as a prized and limited possession to be spent with great care.

One of my dad's dreams was to have a healthy family even while he ministered worldwide. He wrote "family time" on every Monday on our calendar. Usually this meant getting into the car and heading off to dinner somewhere. We spent those evenings talking and joking, then coming home to watch a ball game or do something fun together. Dad achieved his dream: our family remained healthy, and none of his kids rebelled against his values. If it wasn't for family time, I think I would have hated the ministry, felt neglected, and resented my dad for being away. Now, in my own family, we have family time every Thursday night. That's just one example of the power of a well-crafted schedule.

Jesus demonstrated the value of keeping a schedule. The gospel of Luke tells us he regularly went to the synagogue because it was "his custom" (4:16). There he taught people, and his words changed the world. He also had a habit of getting up early to pray. Imagine if he had woken up one morning and said, "I don't feel like going to the synagogue today" or "I don't feel like praying." Thankfully, certain things were on his schedule in ink. He did them because the dream compelled him to. In my view, if keeping a schedule was good enough for Jesus, we are arrogant if we think we can live by our whims and blow off our assignments and appointments. No dreamer treats the limited resource of time we have been given in a disrespectful or casual way.

I've never seen people who are lax with their schedule come out ahead. Often I'll be shaking hands after a service and someone will say, "Hey, Luke, remember me? I used to attend church here, and now I'm back."

"Glad to see you again," I'll say. "What happened?"

The story is always the same.

"I just got lazy about coming," they say. "I started hanging around friends at work. Things got a little crazy. I sort of lost my way."

I can see that their time away usually took them off track. The dream dimmed in their eyes. They experienced a setback on their journey.

Sadly, many people spend much more time planning their vacations than their dreams. So their vacations are awesome, but their dreams drift. Too many people believe in fate—that whatever is destined to happen will happen no matter what. But your destiny is not going to happen by fate. It is not automatic. You won't drift your way there. The hard truth is, it may not happen at all. It depends on you. Such is the awesome, terrifying power of free choice we have been given.

The antidote to drift is a purposeful schedule that connects your dream to your daily life.

Proverbs 21:5 says that "good planning and hard work lead to prosperity" (NLT). And when the Bible uses the word *prosperity,* it always means more than money. It means all aspects of life flourishing as they should. I've noticed that the more I plan, the more prosperous I become. In 2013 when I got hold of my dream, I began to work with others to plan out what we hoped to accomplish. We did it with great humility and prayed together, "God, this is the best plan we can come up with. If you want to change it, go ahead. We will work hard and commit it to you."

That's the kind of attitude God can honor. Choose to become a person who plans a well-thought-out schedule so your dreams take root and bear fruit.

SIMPLE LIFESTYLE

When scheduling your time, keep this next principle at the forefront of your mind: if you pack your calendar, it will crowd out your dream.

Our culture has an addiction to busyness. Adults run around trying to make enough money and have enough fun. Kids are shuttled back and forth to sports and dance practices, school, tutoring, and more. We buy the myth that we don't have enough time. In truth, everyone has plenty of time. We just choose to use it a certain way. Much of it gets wasted on things that only appear productive.

I have observed and experienced a powerful, surprising fact: dreamers live simple lives. They don't overload their schedules. Rather, they choose a lifestyle that makes room for their dreams to flourish. No dream will grow in rushed circumstances.

The CEO of a multibillion-dollar company attends our church. He flies all over the country during the week. But every weekend he serves in our children's ministry. Talk about making time! He may be the busiest guy in our church, but he keeps his life relatively simple so he can fulfill his dream of helping kids.

When we clutter our calendars, we kill our dreams. Worse, we actually cheat people of the benefits of our dreams. We rob the world of that special thing we were designed to do.

What if you looked at your calendar right now and saw your schedule was packed with too much stuff? There's only one way out: start simplifying. Each of us has sown our way into that kind of trap before. Whatever you sow grows. If you have sown busyness and an overly complex life, you will reap the results in fatigue, lack of true productivity, and a diminished dream. It will take time, perhaps months, to fully reverse course and sow instead in the direction of simplicity. But it's better to change the pattern now than to give more of your life to the tyranny of an out-of-control calendar.

Early in my ministry, my dad would say to me on Monday or Tuesday, "You'd better be studying. At 10:45 Sunday morning, the lights come on and the people will be ready for a word."

It took discipline to heed his words, to turn down other things, and to stick with a simple schedule. Often I didn't want to study—but I knew the lights would go up Sunday morning, and I would have nothing to say to the thousands who showed up ready to hear. Even if I'd had a terrible week personally, I sowed during the week for a harvest on Sunday.

Many people think they can sow whatever they want and reap a different harvest. That's like sowing potatoes and expecting watermelons. So many families fill their lives with too much entertainment and leisure, video games, violent movies, lack of sleep, impure thoughts, and work. Then they wonder why their deepest dreams aren't coming to pass. Proverbs 19:3 says that a man makes bad choices, then rages against God when the consequences aren't more favorable. That describes so many in our day. We have the choice where to sow, but once we sow a seed, we have no more say. That harvest will come up whether we like it or not. It's an iron law of nature. What we sow is what will grow. *Truth!*

What harvest do you want in life? A defining dream? Or years of running here and there with no long-term benefit? Take a look at your life to this point. Own what you've sown, cut some things out, and let your schedule reflect your highest dream. *Committing to this Sunday, June 10, 2018.*

DREAMERS FAST

I am convinced that the only way to receive and achieve our highest dreams is through fasting and prayer. By prayer I mean specific set-aside times when we give intensive attention to God and his ideas for us. I have seen the benefits of prayer and fasting time and again.

Years ago my dad asked the church to fast and pray for thirty-one days. We were facing great opportunities, which required a lot of money we didn't have at the time. The church enthusiastically joined in the fast. What happened amazed us. Not only did we get the answer to our primary prayer request, but we also saw things happen we hadn't even asked for! During that fast the Phoenix Swim Club was given outright to a ministry of our church. Only God could do that. Seven young men from that club went on to win medals in the Sydney Summer Olympics. Also during that fast, some contractors approached us with the desire to build

Bethesda Gardens, a retirement center, on the north side of our campus. That was one of my dad's bigger dreams, and it came to pass during that fast.

A few years later my dad had offered $4 million for the Dream Center campus in Los Angeles but needed $2 million to complete the purchase. He had just thirty days to come up with the money. It looked impossible. Nobody really understood what Dad was trying to build there because Dream Centers didn't exist yet. Dad thought he would lose the property, but he and others began fasting and asking God to intervene. Within that time $2 million was donated, leading to the purchase and establishment of the Dream Center, which went on to touch the lives of millions of people. It happened because of fasting and prayer.

Every dream is a partnership between you and God. You can do only so much to make it happen. God must do the rest. I have seen God create a hunger inside me and others to connect with our dream to the point where we want it more than we want food. Fasting is the expression of deep hunger for breakthrough. It's the temporary denial of the flesh to attain a major life goal. It's saying no to yourself to get a yes from God. It renounces the natural to invoke the supernatural.

I'm not sure exactly how it works—but it works.

Normal life for most of us means hearing and obeying our stomachs all day long. My stomach cries out for food, and I respond, "Yes, master. What would you like?" Most of us don't even question it. I know people— like my wife and me—who are so driven by appetite sometimes that we see a commercial for a certain hamburger on television at night and then, still in our pajamas, drive to that restaurant to get one. That's how much we have an appetite for it. We go completely out of our way to satisfy that hunger. (Don't judge!)

Good food is a blessing, but there are seasons when God wants our attention. He wants to speak to us about important things. At those *yes*

times, he wants us to focus our appetites on him. Fasting gets God's attention like food gets ours. What food does for us, fasting does for him. It satisfies him. It makes him want to respond.

When we fast and declare that the cry of our souls is greater than the cry of our bellies, God responds. Only he can address the hunger of the soul. Fasting feeds our relationship with God. It reminds us that there's more to us than what we see and helps us attain God's perspective. People spend so much time on the run, nickel-and-diming God, rather than giving him the best of their schedule and attention. He asks, *Are you willing to set aside time to seek my ideas? Are you willing to put aside even food for a few hours or days?*

Jesus said that his followers would fast. In Matthew 6:16 Jesus said, "When you fast." Not "if" but "when." There was an assumption by Jesus that we would fast and pray. He connected the idea of closeness with God to fasting. Many people don't fast because they don't believe it will help. I've heard so many people say, "I've got a brain, and God expects me to use it." They dismiss God's supernatural participation in our dream. Yes, we use our natural gifts to get things done, but without divine direction, our brains will work against us, not for us. Our dream will remain limited and frustrated. *So true, I agree!*

It's hard but true: in this life, every dream must die before it lives. Every seed "dies" before it sprouts. Jesus himself died before being raised up to new life. Fasting is a picture of death to self. It tells God, "Unless you are involved, my dream will never happen." It takes us to the end of our rope, where God says, "I've gotcha! Now I'll bring your dreams to life." His goal is to take us light-years ahead in our businesses, our families, our dreams. But we must appeal to him. James 4:10 says when we go low in front of God, he will lift us up. Fasting is a way of bowing before God in respect and surrender.

A man named Ezra was leading a defenseless people across a desert, totally exposed and with many enemies along the way. He had bragged about God's power and protection to the king of Persia. Now he needed God to come through. What did he do? He called a fast. A whole nation humbled itself before God. They afflicted their souls with self-denial. They prioritized the spiritual over the physical. They made themselves small in their own eyes and made God big. As a result they traveled safely through the desert against great odds. Fasting brought protection and power that no enemy could overcome (see Ezra 8:21–23).

If you are serious about dream-centered living and leadership, I urge you to consider fasting. So many people want to live casually, have a wonderful life, and invite God in occasionally to help them. That's not the dreamer's path. Dreamers pay the price to get God's attention and satisfy his desire for partnering closely with them. I can say with confidence that without fasting, our church and my life would not be experiencing the extraordinary things we are today. I would not be writing this book. I might not even be pursuing my calling anymore. Fasting has been that important for our journey.

There are many books about fasting and many different kinds of fasts. I'll mention just a few:

- The John Wesley fast goes for twenty-four hours starting at lunchtime. You miss dinner and breakfast and eat lunch the next day.
- A liquid fast is just that—liquids, such as juices, only—and usually lasts just a few days.
- A Daniel fast like the one I did involves eating only things that grow from the ground.
- Some people's biggest craving is media or sports or whatever. Give up that thing for a while. Let God help you know what to abstain from.

One more tip: if possible, have a partner to fast and pray with. It's a lot easier to go through the difficult moments with the solidarity and encouragement of a buddy.

In my view, an annual fast is absolutely necessary to dream-centered leadership. We usually fast as a staff and church at the end of the year. Every time it brings heightened sensitivity and gets us focused again on the important things.

DREAMERS GET QUIET AND LISTEN

Fasting doesn't help much if we don't get quiet and listen. I encourage people to take a few vacation days, go somewhere beautiful, put away the distractions, and set the stage for something good to happen.

And then listen.

You might use the words I said over and over: *God, give me a dream.* Then sit for a while and say nothing. Isaiah 30:15 tells us that in quietness and trust we find strength. It's not the quietness that strengthens us; it's what we hear in those times. God speaks very quietly most of the time because he wants to find people who will listen. I was amazed how much I heard God, and how confident I was it was him, during my forty-day fast. I realized he had probably been speaking to me all along, but I hadn't slowed down enough to recognize or hear his voice.

You may discover that certain habits seem to be hindering your ability to hear God. Maybe an addiction to something, a compulsive need to check social media or texts, out-of-control anger, or some other habit you know is hurting you and your relationships. God will often put his finger on that thing first because it muddies the waters. The Bible says our sins—the ones we insist on holding on to—will cut us off from God unless we renounce them (see Psalm 66:18). He is not angry. He's just waiting until we want him more than the habit. If you find that you're not hearing anything at all during your quiet times, ask him to reveal any areas that need to change. He will surely speak to you.

Some quiet times are just that—quiet. I may sense God's presence but hear nothing specific. Other times I feel like I hear nothing at all. It's not uncommon for me to find myself in quiet time wondering, *What do I do now? I feel like a fool just sitting here. I don't hear anything. How do I proceed?* I do a few simple things to give those moments some structure. One is based on the acronym ACTS, which stands for Adoration, Confession, Thanksgiving, and Supplication.

- Adoration is loving God for who he is. Simply put, it's adoring God. It's worship, acknowledging his qualities and goodness. You can speak this or sing it to music. When I give God adoration, my attitude always changes. My heart connects with the truth of the words I am speaking. It's an uplifting experience every time.

- Confession is telling him what we have done wrong, asking for forgiveness, and pledging to leave those things behind. I often find that adoration flows into confession as I see the infinite difference between God's perfection and my own imperfections. Confession really is good for the soul, as the saying goes. I always feel lighter and freer once I throw off the weights.

- Thanksgiving flows, too, as I thank him for anything and everything that comes to mind. I know one man who committed to thanking God for something new every day. He said not only does he never run out of topics, but he also thinks of far more to thank God for than he even intends. Thanking God is one of the most satisfying things we can do. I try to stay in thanking mode not just during quiet time but all through the day.

- Supplication means asking. This is when we put our requests in front of him. Notice that in this ACTS exercise we do this last. Some people rush to God with a list of things they want. He is gracious and will often answer those requests, but the Bible says he also knows what we need before we ask him (see Matthew 6:8). I like the fact that supplication comes last because it means my primary purpose for coming to God is not to receive but to honor him.

ACTS helps me stay focused after I have been quiet for a while. My goal in each of these activities is to hear God if he speaks to me. Reading the Bible also helps me hear God. Reading Scriptures does amazing things for your life, even if you haven't embraced faith yet. For me, sometimes the words on the page take on special meaning for my circumstance. I know that God is highlighting them for me, so it becomes a dialogue between us. Other times I am simply inspired, cautioned, or taught by what I read.

I also keep a journal of what I think I hear during these times. This practice has been more helpful than I imagined because when I go back and read parts of the journal, I see how my dreams came to pass, my struggles were overcome, and my requests were answered. I write my goals down as requests and statements of confidence about what God will do. Sometimes I gain clarity on a dream just by writing it out. God uses it to move me forward. I journal especially in seasons when I'm trying to hear God about specific things. I don't pressure myself to write something every day.

This leads us to one of the most common questions I hear from people: How do I know if I'm hearing God? First, I am convinced that "God nudges" come into our minds all the time. I think everyone hears from God, though most of us ignore or dismiss what we hear or attribute what God tells us to our own imaginations. So how do we know which nudges are from God? After all, some nudges are authored in hell, not heaven. Here are some signposts and guardrails that help us recognize God's nudges and steer clear of those that aren't from God:

His Nudges Are Always Consistent with the Bible

God does not contradict himself. He's not going to tell you to leave your family or cheat on a business deal. It seems obvious, but some people delude themselves into believing that God is calling them to do something wrong. "He told me to leave my wife and marry this younger woman!" they might say. That's not a God nudge.

If the Nudge Is Contrary to Everything Else in Your Life, Be Wary

If it goes against your gifting and talents, against the advice of every friend and relative, even against your own truest dreams, watch out. Ask people around you, "Does this sound like me? Can you see me doing this?" The Bible says we should always seek counsel before doing anything big (see Proverbs 11:14). Sometimes God's voice comes through those around us, so it's critical to invite their advice.

Over the years a number of PGA tour members have attended our church. One man in particular always talked about quitting the tour to become a pastor. My dad and I discouraged him. We told him, "God gave you a platform to share the gospel on a worldwide stage through professional golf." He protested, "I don't want to do that. I want to preach and teach." We heard him preach and teach and said, "Keep golfing!"

This man went into a dream-seeking time, and God spoke to him and said, *I don't want you to quit the PGA tour. I want you to look at the three hundred guys on the tour a little differently. I want you to be their pastor. I want you to shepherd the people you rub shoulders with every week. Love them, serve them, lead them to faith.* It was a huge revelation to him. He stayed on the PGA tour and now goes into work with new energy knowing God is using him to influence the guys there.

Quick, Frenzied Nudges Don't Usually Come from God

God's nudges promote peace and patience, even if they require our action. If you feel pressured to take quick action based on fear, that's not from God.

Sometimes He Just Wants Conversation

There will be times when God whispers to you for no other reason than to talk with you. Sometimes his purpose is purely personal. It's a powerful reality and reflects the reason he made us way back in the beginning: to walk and talk with him like friends.

His Nudges Call Us to Acts of Service, Sacrifice, and Faith

I have found that Satan's nudges are fairly easy to detect. They are usually self-promoting and self-serving. Too many people follow only nudges that promise quick prosperity, a new job position, or something else, even at the expense of uprooting their families or walking away from their real dreams.

Be honest: How many people do you know who leave one job for another with less responsibility, fewer benefits, and less prestige because they felt a nudge from God? How quickly we call it a promotion when a "nudge" requires us to move far away, unravel relationships, throw our lives out of balance, and start over again—all for an attractive raise, a bigger house, or a better climate. I'm not saying these things never happen. But when you look around and everyone is talking about how God promoted and prospered them every single time, there is reason to be suspicious about whether or not they are hearing from God or following their own desires.

The record of history and the Bible is that nudges aren't always pleasant. The Holy Spirit nudged the apostle Paul again and again to go to Jerusalem and assured him he would be taken captive there. That kind of nudge would thin the ranks, don't you think?

God the Father nudged Jesus about going to the cross. Many of the disciples died martyrs' deaths. Abraham was told to sacrifice his son Isaac. On and on it goes.

Nearly forty years ago, God nudged my dad to leave a church of four thousand people he had built in Davenport and go to a small church in Arizona. I remember well when he sat us down in the living room of our home in Iowa and said, "We are going to go to a church that is about one twentieth the size of our church here. It's going to be tough. It's going to be starting all over again. It's going to be less of a salary. We'll have to struggle for a little while. But I have heard from God, and we're going."

I was ten years old and thinking, *Why are we doing this? We've got it made here.* I didn't want that nudge to be true!

Now I can better sense when a nudge is from the Holy Spirit, and I know that I often have to humble myself, encourage somebody, or give something away. Not every nudge from him will be painful or unpleasant, but expect some to require gut-wrenching decisions. Some will test your commitment to your dream. Some will force you to decide what is most important in life. Some will even bring discomfort and apparent loss of reputation or position.

The good news is that Jesus went there first, and there's always something good on the other side of those painful nudges. Jesus agonized in the garden of Gethsemane because his Father was asking him to carry a cross before he wore a crown. Some nudges will demand we do the same.

Sometimes He Nudges Us to Test Our Trust in Him

When we obey a nudge that doesn't feel great, it's our way of loving God more than ourselves. I wouldn't trade those moments for all the money in the world. That's when all our talk becomes real. It's just you and God—and he knows, and you know, and he knows you know, and you know he knows you know! You have no one to hide from, nothing to fake. When you follow the nudge when no one is looking, it's one of the great victories of your life.

I find that I am rarely 100 percent certain that a nudge is from God. I don't think anyone has that kind of clarity. But when you've run it through the grid and feel confident it's him, act on the nudge. Faith is spelled R-I-S-K. God won't punish you for sincerely seeking him and then making a mistake. If you step wrong, he'll rescue and redeem that situation. He's good that way.

To make sure I'm hearing his nudges as best I can, I try to keep the line open and clear between my ear and his voice. I do this with a few simple habits:

- Instead of listening to a news station on the way to work, with people yelling and speaking harshly about their biased opinions, I listen to music or teaching that promotes peace and love in my heart. It really makes a difference what kind of mood or frame of mind I'm in when I arrive at work. It also keeps the clutter out of my mind so I can be sensitive to God's leadings throughout the day.

- While working or in meetings, I invite God to whisper into my heart and inspire thoughts and words. I ask him, *Is there anything you want to say to me going into this meeting? If you want to give me a creative idea, I'm listening. If you want to drop some wisdom into my mind, go for it. I'm here.*

- While doing administrative work, I keep a notepad nearby. Many times the Lord will drop a person into my mind, maybe someone I know is struggling. I write the name on that pad and get back to work. At my first break I pray for the person, write an encouraging letter, or pick up the phone and call him or her. The more I listen, the more I sense God's nudges and wisdom in everything I do.

- I keep certain symbols in my office that remind me of who I am and the dreams I am pursuing. The golden baton Dad gave me is a symbol of the leadership assignment I have and the history of our family and the church. It often inspires me to breathe a simple prayer: *God, help me to be the leader I need to be. Give me wisdom to lead this church the way the people deserve.*

    Also in my office is a little statue of a fisherman. It reminds me that my primary responsibility is to be a fisher of men and to lead a church that shares the good news with others. We are not to be a spiritual ghetto or country club. The statue reminds me that our assignment is to take life and joy to our community in so many ways.

Will you take the time to sit and listen for God's nudges? Will you prioritize this time in your day? Are you hungry enough for your dream to pay the price of fasting from food? Entertainment? Pleasure? Will you sacrifice a few vacation days to sit someplace beautiful with a Bible and notebook and beg God for a dream? Are you serious enough to go to some close friends and ask them to pray with you that God gives you a burning vision for the next phase of your life? Every dreamer must do these things. Sometimes in those moments, God will give you a different dream. Sometimes he will affirm the one he already gave you. Sometimes he will add to it.

The value of the dream will far surpass whatever price you pay to discover it.

Here are some important points for effective dreamers:

- Make a schedule and craft your calendar. It's critical to direct your time rather than just floating along hoping for the best.
- Banish the clutter. A packed schedule will crowd out a dream every time. Trim your commitments and focus on what is truly important.
- Fast and pray at least annually. Experience has taught me that dreams are not fully realized until we practice denying ourselves so we can better hear and perceive God's dream for our lives. There is no substitute.
- Put aside mental distractions often to spend time with God. That's when we feel his nudges, which can include new, exciting directions for our dreams.

7

The Habits
of Dreamers

I was standing on the edge of a sixty-foot cliff, petrified. Below me were the lake and our party of boats and Jet Skis bobbing around. Friends hollered up at me.

"Just jump, Luke! It's been forty minutes already!"

"Yeah, jump, you chicken!" my wife chimed in. She is always so helpful.

Everyone else had climbed up these rocks and jumped several times, whooping all the way down. But I felt like my legs were stone. Even if I wanted to take the plunge, my body was in full rebellion.

"Give me a minute," I shouted down to a new chorus of groans. Here was their fearless leader, stuck high up on the ledge.

It had started with people jumping off relatively low rocks—ten feet, fifteen feet, then twenty feet above the water. I could handle that, with some trepidation. Then my brother, Matthew, climbed up higher. I saw his body plummeting through the air, almost like he was flying.

That took a long time for him to hit, I thought. *I could never do that. I'd be pondering my mortal existence all the way down.*

Of course, the next person up there was Angel. She is an incredible woman, and she's not afraid to take massive risks. She had already bungee jumped at the state fair, which I thought was nuts simply because she let the carnies hook her up.

Now she flew off the cliff, hollering with joy. Others scrambled up to take the really high jump, and I felt pressure to join them. It was a pretty easy climb up. I reached that hot, baking rock and looked over.

Whoa! That looks much farther down than I imagined, I thought.

That place became my platform of shame for the next forty-five minutes. Other people climbed up and jumped off again several times, but I just stood there. The longer I delayed, the harder it got. I thought of climbing back down, but climbing down is always more dangerous than climbing up. I was stuck.

After a while, people actually got mad at me.

"Come on, Luke!" someone yelled impatiently.

I was holding them all up. I had used all my jokes already, like, "The Bible says, 'Lo, I will be with you always.' Low, not high." They were tired of my stalling tactics.

I saw Angel climbing back up to where I was. She had jumped a couple of times already.

"It's easy," she said. "Just follow me off. Like this."

Over the edge she went for a third time, her war whoop echoing around the lake.

Why on earth am I up here? I asked myself. *I'm starting to feel ridiculous.* I actually wanted to experience the exhilaration they were all feeling, to enjoy those moments of free fall. But it looked like certain death.

Finally, in a moment of foolishness or valiant determination, I stepped off the cliff. Gravity sucked me down, and it felt like minutes passed before my feet hit the water. As I came to the surface I had one thought: *I have got to do that again. In fact, I want to spend the rest of the day jumping off that high ledge.*

Just to note that my fear wasn't without reason, when we got back to the hotel room, one of our guys was in pain. It turned out he had cracked his tailbone by hitting the water wrong. Later, after he had healed, he still claimed the jump was worth it.

Dreamers are risk-takers. You can't separate the two. Dreaming and taking risks come as a package, at least if you want your dream to become a reality. I know that some people are naturally drawn to risk more than others—that's just a fact. But *anyone* can become a risk-taker just like anyone can become a dreamer. It's a learnable skill. It's a choice we make. In fact, it's a must. The dream-centered life involves risk. Dreaming is not simply hearing from God and successfully implementing what you heard. There will be unknown obstacles, gray areas, surprises both good and bad, letdowns, setbacks, comebacks, steep cliffs, calm seas, highs, lows, and everything in between.

That's the nature of risk, but through it all we will never feel more alive.

One of the huge benefits of becoming a risk-taker is that it drives fear out of our lives. Taking risks and experiencing consequences, both successful and unsuccessful, is the best way to defeat fear. You see, fear lurks around trying to immobilize you the way it immobilized me up on that rock. The goal of fear is your inaction. Dreams die that way.

The only way to be dream centered, and really the only way to be fully human, is to regularly defeat fear by taking risks and accomplishing hard things. If we shrink from hard things, we become less human. But when we face a fearful situation and take action, we feel a surge of satisfaction. It may require something like having a difficult conversation with a boss, a spouse, a parent, or a friend. Wrestling addictive behavior and making the courageous decision to bring it into the light. Putting money or reputation or time at risk for a good cause. All these things cause us to feel alive because they banish fear and show faith in a dream.

Dreams and risk always involve feeling some fear. I've taught over the years that courage is not the absence of fear but the willingness to take action in spite of fear. Mark Twain once said, "Courage is resistance to fear, mastery of fear—not absence of fear." In other words, we don't overcome the feeling of fear, but we banish the power it has in our lives.

Jesus asked a number of people to take the risk of following him. One rich young ruler said no and then disappeared completely from the Bible. Did he ever reflect on the day that carpenter rabbi challenged him to give it all away and follow him? What would life have been like if he'd said yes to Jesus? As best we can tell, this man's life went on as it had before. He enjoyed his riches, he grew older, his power faded, and he died.

But had he truly risked anything?

When we don't take fearful risks, we die a little on the inside. Do that enough and it becomes your life pattern. You begin to see yourself as someone who can't cope with challenges and who makes excuses for not risking anything. Instead of strength, resolve, and confidence, your life is characterized by shallowness and a low view of yourself. As life goes on, what-ifs become what-might-have-beens. Your existence may seem comfortable and normal in many ways. But by avoiding risk and fear, you actually avoid your dream and choose the low path of merely existing.

When I was twelve, my family took a vacation to Puerto Vallarta. I was so mesmerized by parasailing I told my dad I wanted to do it. I had the choice of going up four hundred feet, six hundred feet, or eight hundred feet in the air.

"I think I want to go four hundred feet up," I told Dad as I signed up to do it. He nudged me and said, "I think you should go for the eight hundred feet. It's going to be over in ten minutes, and you'll have this experience for the rest of your life. You may as well get everything you can out of it. Besides, if you fall at four hundred feet you'll get maimed, but if you fall at eight hundred feet you'll be dead."

That's Barnett humor again. But Dad was doing me a favor. He was passing his courage to me. He was telling me that risk is okay.

Some people pass fear to the next generation instead. That is the highest cost of avoiding risk. You can handicap your own children with fear. Do your kids and friends look at you and see a courageous person? A risk-taker? A dreamer? Or a safety addict?

The apostle Paul lost his job, was isolated from friends, lived in a strange country, was arrested on trumped-up charges, was beaten and jailed, lived with the constant possibility of martyrdom, and had to put up with people trashing his reputation. Guess what he wrote to a group of friends? "I can do all things through [Christ] who strengthens me" (Philippians 4:13). Wow. Paul embraced risk and reaped huge blessings, not least of which was an amazing absence of the power of fear in his life.

Can you imagine living without being controlled by fear? I imagine Paul waking up every day and saying, "Some good things are going to happen to me today and some bad things, but it doesn't matter because I'm in God's care and I can do all things through Christ who gives me strength." That's the kind of person I want to be.

I have noticed God's kindness: he never gives us challenges too big for us to handle. The battle is always the size of our ability. We don't need all the courage required to finish our dreams; we just need enough to start them. We will grow into our dreams over time as we take risks in following him. I can assure you, none of us have the courage to complete our dreams when we start. Most of us don't even know the extent of them until they unfold before our eyes. We have a million questions, nagging fears, ignorance, and immaturity.

That's okay. We need only one thing: the courage to take the first step. When I answered the call to preach that night in Goodyear, Arizona, I could not fathom all that God would do from there. I didn't need to. I needed to take only one step. The same is true of you as you embrace the dream-centered life.

DREAMERS FIGHT EVERY ROUND

Some years ago I tuned in to a boxing match that was in the eleventh round. One guy was getting beaten to an absolute pulp. His face was swollen, cut, and blood streaked. He looked like he had been ridden hard and put up wet. I felt bad for him. As the final bell sounded, he fell to the canvas and was literally saved by the bell from losing the fight. But when they announced the winner, the referee raised this boxer's hand. I couldn't believe it. The guy looked like a mess. How could he have won? What I didn't see were the ten rounds prior to the final two. He had fought well in those rounds and won the overall victory.

There's a powerful lesson in that. Our dream will not be judged successful or unsuccessful based on one or two rounds but on our entire lives. We're almost guaranteed to lose some rounds, but that's never the whole story.

I think again of the apostle Paul, a guy who lost the early rounds big-time. The first time Paul (at that point called Saul) was ever mentioned in the Bible, he was holding the coats of guys who were killing a Christian named Stephen. They didn't want their clothes to get blood and dirt on them as they murdered Stephen by throwing rocks at him. Acts 8:1 says that Saul approved of their killing him. The next time Saul popped up, he was dragging men and women out of their homes and throwing them into prison (verse 3). He worked hard to be the foremost terrorist attacking the early Christian church. His name inspired caution or fear even in the apostles.

I'd call that losing some early rounds. It's hard to imagine a worse human being than Saul.

Fortunately for everyone, Saul's course changed in a radical way. In the middle rounds of his life, Saul (now Paul) became zealous for God and God's dream for his life. He preached powerfully. Many lives were changed and improved because of him. He found himself on the winning side of his dream.

Then came another difficult round. On Paul's first missionary journey, he got upset with a young traveling companion named John Mark. John Mark wanted to go home early, and Paul had no patience for that. So when Paul's buddy, Barnabas, insisted on taking John Mark with them on a later journey, Paul balked: "No way. That guy's a flake. He bailed on us once and he'll do it again." Paul and Barnabas got into such an awful fight that they parted ways, and the Bible never indicates that they made up.

I'd call that a failure of leadership. Yet Paul went on to write many letters that are now included in the Bible. On the heels of a few lost rounds, Paul bounced back. By the end of his life, he was able to say confidently, "I have fought the good fight" (2 Timothy 4:7).

He lost a number of rounds badly, but he won the match.

The same was true of Moses, David, Abraham, and every other Bible hero. They all won some rounds and lost others. Yet God is so kind to judge us favorably. He called Moses his servant and spoke to him like a dear friend. He called David "a man after my heart" (Acts 13:22). Abraham was known as a friend of God (see 2 Chronicles 20:7). Noah was dubbed "a herald of righteousness" (2 Peter 2:5). Each man had major failings in some early, middle, or late rounds. But God judges us on the whole fight of our lives, not those bad rounds.

Jack Wallace was a talented athlete who barely missed the Olympics as a young man. He came to Phoenix First and loved ministry so much that he studied it and became a pastor of singles for some years. Jack remained in physical pain from his former athletic career and began taking prescription drugs. He became addicted and slipped into alcoholism as well. The middle rounds got rough. One day he stood before our congregation and admitted the double life he was leading. He chose to go through a yearlong restoration process and completed it successfully. My dad helped Jack become pastor of a church in Detroit, and with his leadership it grew to thousands of people. One day Jack flew to Europe to speak, and when he walked off the plane, he fell to the ground and died of a heart attack. Jack Wallace lost some middle rounds, but God will say he won the match.

Maybe you've seen some hard rounds. But no judge renders a verdict while the fight is still in progress. As long as you're breathing, the dream is alive. You're not allowed to judge yourself yet. First Corinthians 4:5 says emphatically to withhold our own judgment and let God judge when it's time. There is always time to rebound, to get up off the mat and start swinging.

Maybe you have a hot temper but are also generous. Or maybe you're stubborn but also very kind. God sees all of who we are, not just our bad traits. He doesn't demand perfection, just commitment to keep going. His merciful judgment will remember our good more than our bad.

My friend Henry is a mixed-martial-arts fighter, one of the best in the world. He grew up in a family of seven kids with a dad who chose alcohol and drugs over his family. Henry became, by his own description, a very selfish person. He liked the sport of wrestling because it was one-on-one combat. He thought his purpose in life, his dream, was to be the best in the world. He achieved that dream and became known by millions. He was a gold medalist at the 2008 Olympics and undefeated in mixed martial arts.

Then Henry was scheduled to fight another man for the Ultimate Fighting Championship. The fight didn't last long; Henry was knocked out in the first round. He told me later, "Losing in the first round of the championship in some sense was discouraging and hurtful, not just physically but the emotional side of things."

But Henry had changed dreams. When he became a champion, he realized it was empty without an even greater purpose for living. "It's not until it actually hits you that 'Hey, man, this is something that's temporary. Life isn't about you,'" he said. "I call it JOY. Jesus, Others, and You. Before, it was the other way around. Things tend to change, and through the pain that I've gone through, it's produced passion for Christ."

In the wake of his highly publicized loss, Henry told me he looked to the example of Paul, who was in a prison in Rome and still wrote, "I can do all things through [Christ] who strengthens me" (Philippians 4:13).

"He's suffering, but he's content with what God has given him," Henry told me. "He wants more, but he's content because he's giving it his all. I'm in that similar situation where I can do all things through Christ who strengthens me. When I lost the fight, I didn't lose the battle. I think there are bigger things for me than just the cage, championships, rings, or gold medals. It's using the platform God has given me for the greater good."

Today Henry shares the gospel with his audiences. "I just use the platform that God has given me," he told our church. "I really just fight for the mic, for the camera, to inspire those who are lost, who believe it's just about money, fame, and maybe women or drugs. I'm able to captivate and fight in front of twenty-five thousand people. I'm able to share who Jesus Christ is and what he's done. That's what I look forward to, not so much the fight, but what I'm able to do after the fight that's going to make this world a better place."

That's an inspiring perspective.

I have another friend, Jim Bakker, who was one of the most well-known Christian personalities in the 1980s. Jim went to prison, convicted on charges of fraud. He had also cheated on his wife, and his worldwide ministry collapsed in a matter of months. He went from being on television screens in millions of homes to being a number in the federal prison system. It was one of the most dramatic falls I have ever witnessed.

In 1997 I was a pastor in Dayton, Ohio, when Jim was released from prison. He had served eight or nine years. I asked him to come preach at my church and give his testimony of what God had done in his heart during his incarceration. He had been out of prison only a week or so when he arrived at the airport. My brother, Matthew, was with me in Dayton for a few days, so we picked Jim up together. As we were walking from the airport terminal to the parking lot, someone recognized Jim and yelled, "Burn in hell, Jim Bakker! Burn in hell!" Then he sped off. Matthew, who's as competitive and loyal as I am, started chasing the car on foot, yelling, "Get back here, punk!" He wanted a piece of that guy.

Jim's flight had been delayed, and the church service was in progress when we arrived. There were a hundred or so people there who were not happy that I was having Jim speak. The moment I introduced him, they stood to their feet and filed out to make a point of protest. I thought, *That's not how the people of God behave.*

Jim stayed his course and now is being used in a whole new way. In 1998, while working in the LA Dream Center, Jim met Lori Graham and they were married. In 2002, Jim and Lori adopted five children from inner-city Phoenix where Lori had ministered for years. Today the whole family is involved in producing *The Jim Bakker Show,* an hour-long daily broadcast aired around the world.

Jim didn't quit, even when the middle rounds looked absolutely devastating. He learned how to deal with the failures and then forget those former rounds. He centered his life around a dream, not fear or failure.

Always keep in mind that whatever happened in your past does not have to determine the outcome of the rounds you're in now. You're alive.

You're fighting. Those other rounds are in the rearview mirror. Keep swinging.

THE GRACE OF ADVERSITY

I have learned that God intends us to fight battles because adversity is what makes us great. It reveals what we're made of. It shows us how great we can be. Some of you may recall a boxer named Evander Holyfield. Holyfield never got his due respect until he fought champion Mike Tyson. Holyfield was undersized, underestimated. When he faced Tyson, he came out wearing a belt that quoted Philippians 4:13. The fight wasn't even close: Holyfield mopped the ring with Tyson, to everyone's surprise. In the eleventh round, he knocked Tyson down for good. After the fight, Tyson said it was a fluke and could never happen again. So they fought a second time, and Holyfield was doing so well that in the third round, Tyson grabbed him and took a big bite out of the cartilage of his ear. Today, most sports fans remember that fight as one of the legendary moments in boxing.

If not for that great adversity, Holyfield would have been a journeyman fighter, quickly forgotten even as a champion. He needed Mike Tyson and that memorable, painful ear bite! The bite didn't make him great, but it put a spotlight on his greatness.

The feeling of fear will often visit us in the dream-centered life. Courage is taking the risk anyway. As I mentioned before, I still have a potential stuttering problem today. Before I go up to preach, I feel that anxiety. I have decided it's good for me to feel that fear. It forces me to lean on God's power, not my own. It helps push away pride. It focuses me on the dream, which makes the risk worth it.

It also causes me to have greater grace for people around me. Knowing I'm not perfect helps me to believe in others when I see their flaws and failures. If you never had fear or failings, you'd be insufferable! You'd be judgmental. You can always tell a perfectionist by how he or she treats others. If you don't give yourself grace and encouragement, you won't give it to others. The more you experience grace, the more you have to give.

Forget those past rounds. Use that energy to fight the round you're in now.

DREAMERS DECLARE

One of the bravest things a dreamer can do is announce the dream to others. When God downloaded those five ideas to me, I became fearful. I bargained with him: *God, can we keep these things between you and me? I mean, what if they don't come to pass? You and I will both look bad. Besides, people might challenge my motives. It's much safer if this stuff stays between you and me. How about you make them happen over the next ten years without my sharing them with anybody?*

His answer was no surprise: *Luke, secret faith is shallow faith. Share the dream.*

I'm convinced that until you hear the dream coming out of your mouth, you haven't embraced and believed it. It's dormant and will not happen. It must be spoken and shared.

Because I overcame the power of fear and shared the dream, nearly all those dreams went into motion within months. Had I not declared that dream, there's no way it would have happened. I would have stagnated and shrunk back into my own small thinking. Now those dreams are pushing me! I hear them inspiring me from the mouths of others. They compel me to put forth effort in every aspect of my work. I actually have to keep growing to keep up with the dreams. The same will happen to you when you courageously declare your dream to other people.

Dreamers Serve Others

My kindergarten teacher was Miss Zehnger. One day a classmate brought an injured pigeon in from the playground. Instead of throwing the bird out, Miss Zehnger surprised us by buying a cage for it and making it our class pet. She let us feed the bird. After a while its wing healed, and one day Miss Zehnger said, "Come outside with me. I want to show you something you'll never forget."

We followed as she marched outside with the cage, opened the cage door, and waited. The pigeon didn't budge. He seemed to like his new house. Miss Zehnger shook and tapped the cage, and the pigeon finally hopped forward, looked over the edge, and flew away.

Perhaps without knowing it, Miss Zehnger gave us a picture in that moment of how to be a dream releaser. Each of us can tap on people's cages and say, "You're meant for more than this. You can fly."

My brother, Matthew, is a man of great power and faith, the pastor of the LA Dream Center. But it wasn't always that way. He was a nervous kid who chewed his nails to the stubs. He was always the last kid in line because kids would push him around a little. He was passive in a lot of ways. But one day my dad looked at this little boy and said, "Matthew, you can do a lot more with your life than you think you can. I'd like you to start by playing Pop Warner football. Just see if you like it."

The first game of the season was so boring. The score was 0 to 0 with three seconds left. Matthew's team was on their own one-yard line. Matthew was playing the position of running back. Dad and I stood on the sidelines hoping they would down it and get a tie, rather than hand it off and get tackled in the end zone for a safety.

Instead, on the last play the quarterback pitched the ball to Matthew six yards deep in the end zone. A guy hit him in the end zone, which would have lost them the game, but Matthew broke the tackle, spun around, turned the corner, broke another tackle, and ran down the sidelines.

"Run, Matthew! Run!" Dad yelled, running down the sideline with him. I ran after them both, amazed at what I was seeing. Matthew scored the winning touchdown.

If ever there are moments that change a life, that was one of them. Matthew went on to be the state champion wrestler three years in a row, all because Dad tapped his cage and said, "You can be more than you think you can."

The Bible says we receive authority to build people up, not tear them down (see Ephesians 4:11–12). Each of us has some level of authority at work, in a family, or at school. That authority is given to build others up. We can use it to tear dreams down or to build dreams up. We will receive as much authority as we will use to build people up.

When Matthew turned seventeen, Dad tapped his cage again and said, "I think it's time for you to pastor your first church."

Matthew said, "Do you think I can?"

With that, Dad shipped him off to a rough neighborhood of Los Angeles to help him start the Dream Center. That amazing story is still being written. Mark Twain said, "Really great people make you feel that you, too, can become great." That statement has proven itself time and again in my family.

In the Bible a man named Joseph had big dreams but found himself in a dungeon. While he waited for his dream to be resurrected, he asked a fellow prisoner, "Tell me your dream." I find it amazing that Joseph had his own dream but was interested in someone else's dream. If you're interested only in your own dream, you're thinking too small. Dreaming big means becoming a dream releaser—using your resources, your time, your wealth, your wisdom, and your strength to help others. You know you're on your way to your dream when you are releasing others' dreams.

One of our staff members has a God-sized dream, yet he asks me every day, "Pastor, what can I do for you?" It's amazing how that makes me feel. I know he has big dreams, yet he makes my dreams his priority.

Jesus did that. He helped people see beyond what they were to what they could be. He saw Simon and changed his name to Peter. Peter was an impetuous man. He was always rushing in where angels fear to tread. He was considered unstable and unable to keep his commitments. But Jesus said, "That's not how I see you. I see you as a rock, so I'm going to call you Peter!" Peter literally means "rock."* I want to be that way. I want to see what people can become rather than who they are. I want vision to look beyond their present reputation.

It's a risk to believe in people. Some will prove you wrong. But anybody can believe in people after their success. The risk is to believe in them before they succeed. Tap their cages. Speak that belief. Words inspire. They encourage, which means to instill courage. Words can paint a picture of the dream before it comes to pass. Words are a catalyst for success or failure.

Believe in people and then take your strengths and use them to strengthen others. If you have a strong marriage, help those who need stronger marriages. If you have a college education, help those who would like one. If you have overcome an addiction, help others overcome it too. With the faith you have for your dream, find others who are struggling with theirs and be a dream releaser. There's enough negative talk in the world. Be someone who is known for believing in people.

I was walking to my car after three services one Sunday, and I was worn out. I remember feeling for some reason that I had laid an egg that Sunday. Just then a woman approached me. "You may think this is

---

* John F. Walvoord and Roy B. Zuck, eds., *The Bible Knowledge Commentary: New Testament* (Colorado Springs, CO: David C Cook, 1983), 57.

weird," she said, "but I was driving home after the service and felt prompted to turn around, come back, and tell you that the message today really ministered to me."

She had no idea how bad I was feeling about the message. Her encouragement helped me to get God's view on it. A few small words changed my whole week.

Another time I passed by a woman sitting on the curb with her children, and I felt prompted to go back and talk with her. She said she was homeless and had driven their car to church that day on fumes. I gave her some money and encouraged her to get some food or put gas in the car.

A year later I got a letter from that woman. She said that moment had been a pivotal point in her life. She felt that God didn't care until I stopped and helped her out. She wasn't homeless anymore and was going to nursing school. Her life was on track. All I had done was tap her cage gently. She had flown out and caught the wind of her dream.

Whose cage are you tapping?

DREAMS RUB OFF

Here's the same kind of question, but in reverse: Whose dream is rubbing off on you? Just like my parents did with me, I warned my daughters when they were teenagers, "Be careful who you hang around with. Stupid rubs off."

Actually, everything rubs off, good or bad. At work, if people are productive and happy, you feel more productive and happy. If everyone is using profanity, you probably find yourself using those words too. If greed is the goal, people become greedy. I have even heard that in ultimate fighting matches, more fights break out in the stands between audience members than in the ring itself. Violence rubs off.

I have seen good things rub off at the fitness club. If you go regularly, you see the same people showing up week after week to chase their fitness goals. They're on the treadmills, lifting weights, drinking their protein shakes. I get inspired by that. It's like I have a silent contract with these people, whose names I don't even know, to keep showing up. Fitness rubs off.

Who is rubbing off on you? Whose dream is becoming your dream?

I didn't immediately obey my dad when he dropped me off at college and said, "Luke, please make good friends. Don't associate with fools." But since then I have tried to spend my life being a bridge builder and hanging around bridge builders. It has helped me dramatically. These days I can't stand to be with bomb throwers, people with a low emotional IQ who tear up those around them and don't even feel it in their conscience. I'm so accustomed to being in encouraging environments. I have chosen to hang around with people who have dream-centered lives.

More than twenty-five years ago, a young pastor named Jentezen Franklin sat up in the balcony at one of our church's conferences. He was on the verge of quitting but heard my dad preach about being a prisoner of great expectations. Jentezen began to dream again, went back to his city, and built one of the greatest churches in the world today. It was his discovery of the power of fasting and prayer that so influenced my own life.

A young hippie came to our church back when Dad was just beginning in Phoenix. The man was high on some drug, but God gave him a dream so big it compelled him to leave his addictions. He was the man who took Grand Canyon University public and was one of the catalysts that enabled the university to grow by leaps and bounds today.

Almost thirty years ago my dad was asked to speak at the National Black Pastors Conference. He asked the leaders why they had invited him. "Everyone knows that black pastors are the best preachers in the world," Dad said. "This is not fair! You're setting me up for failure." The leaders said, "We like you. You've got a black heart." I'm not sure what that meant, but Dad took it as a compliment. That day, Dad shared his signature message, "There's a Miracle in Your House." T. D. Jakes, the struggling young pastor of a church of a couple hundred people, was sitting there. Jakes heard that message and later said, "My heart was beating so fast that I thought I was going to have a heart attack." He told himself, "If I get out of here alive, I'm going to go back and be the miracle."

I'll ask again, whose dream is rubbing off on you? Who are you inspiring? Whose cage are you tapping? Who's tapping yours?

Here are some ways to cultivate the habits of a dreamer:

- Fight every round. You might lose some early ones (I know I did), but you can still win the match. If you're alive, you're still in the fight, so keep swinging.
- Declare your dream to those around you. Secret faith is shallow faith. Get it out in the open.
- Release other people's dreams. If you are so focused on your dream that you don't take the time to help or encourage others with their dreams, something is definitely wrong. All effective dreamers take the risk to believe in, invest in, and strengthen the people around them. It's not about *I*; it's about *we.*
- Make friends who push you in the right directions. Stuff rubs off!

8

A Delayed
Dream Arrives

After two and a half years of struggling with the multisite-church dream, I gave it up. "I'm powerless here," I said in exasperation. "I can't make it happen. We're stretched so thin right now with everything we're doing, we can't go out and buy a property unless we know it's the right direction. The timing doesn't feel right yet, so I'm done pushing this for now. If it happens, it won't be because I made it happen."

With that, I quietly put the idea on the back burner. The other four dreams were progressing well enough that putting that dream on hold didn't make me feel like too much of a failure. I thought maybe I had heard wrong during my fast or maybe God was holding back on the idea for reasons I couldn't see.

I was about to see how God works in unexpected ways.

THE BEND IN THE ROAD IS NOT
THE END OF THE ROAD

I had reached a bend in the road, a detour, maybe even a stop sign. I preached often on this subject and now was relearning the lesson in real time—never a fun experience. I knew from past experiences that life's greatest lessons are learned when there is a sudden detour, not on an easy, open highway. The bend in the road may be the greatest friend you have. I now had to embrace that principle anew.

A Brake on Pride

God often slows us down so our pride doesn't get out of control. The apostle Paul wrote that he was given "a thorn . . . in the flesh" to keep him from getting a big head because of his revelations (2 Corinthians 12:7). "Thorn in the flesh" can be translated "stake into my body."* This was no splinter-sized pain. This was like someone driving a pointed stick into your guts. Why so severe? Because God had given Paul tremendous revelation through an actual visit to heaven, and God knew it could lead to Paul's downfall through pride. So he gave him a brake—an unpleasant thing to keep pride from accelerating and ruining Paul's dream. He did it so Paul would keep the right perspective: God's grace and strength are enough. Success and knowledge puff us up, but God wanted to make sure that nobody could explain Paul's wisdom and knowledge in human terms again. That's how big his dream was.

That bend in the road may be a brake on your pride so that when the dream becomes reality, you don't take the credit.

Character Building

Disruptions and delays develop character in us on the way to our dream. They are really the only way to train and strengthen us, to keep us trusting and believing in God's power, not our own. Of course, I would prefer he just made me bulletproof and weatherproof and put me in the battle,

---

* Alexander Souter, *A Pocket Lexicon to the Greek New Testament* (London: Oxford University Press, 1917), 231–232, 237.

but God doesn't work that way. Instead he takes time to build our character through discipline, as he did with Paul.

God doesn't sugarcoat his dream-building processes. He says, *You want to be a dreamer? Good. I'm going to treat you as a son or daughter. All good parents care enough to discipline and shape the character of their children. It might hurt, but it's worth it. Ready? Here we go.*

When we enter a season of what feels like unreasonable difficulty and chastisement, it's not because God is rejecting us. Rather, it's proof he is taking us seriously and preparing us for the fulfillment of the great dream within us. The danger is that we become angry or discouraged during the discipline. I've heard people say time and again, "I can't believe God would let this happen to me. He must hate me." The Bible addresses this directly, telling us, "Don't shrug off God's discipline. Stand up tall, put your shoulders back, and say, 'I really am a child of God! This hardship proves it'" (see Hebrews 12:6).

Our great comfort is that God is with us every step of the way. We're never alone, even when we feel alone. He also will not give us more than we can handle. Only divine discipline is strong enough to train dreamers for the responsibility of living in their dreams. Disruptive detours are divine disciplines. Interruptions contain instructions. Don't despise those hard spots or get discouraged. Say, "I'm going to be the best student there is. I'm going to come out of this wiser, more knowledgeable, and more determined."

That unexpected bend in the road is going to change you. You will come out of it different. You will pray differently, treat people differently, even dream differently. Some say, "What a morbid outlook! You should be more optimistic." Those are people who don't learn from life's painful lessons. Their optimism is simply false hope and pain avoidance under another name. I am completely optimistic that God will see you through any challenge and use everything you go through in life for the glory of your dream.

Proof of Endurance

Many of us can handle hard trials if they are brief. But delay can feel impossible to endure.

I've learned that everything in life, including the fulfillment of every dream, takes longer than we expect. I am wired to be impatient like everyone else. I want to see things happen right away. But I've seen enough to know that the fulfillment of dreams will often be delayed.

There is great comfort in King David's experience, so vividly captured in many of the songs he wrote. Those lyrics have been passed down to us in the Bible's book of Psalms. Read just a couple, and you see that David often started a psalm with a sigh and ended it with a song. In Psalm 13 he felt forgotten by God, as if God were hiding from him. David was the king in waiting. The great prophet Samuel already had anointed him three times to confirm this future. Yet it was fifteen years until David ascended the throne! Have you waited that long for your dream?

Psalm 13 captures a moment when Israel's army was chasing David across the wilderness to kill him. He didn't have a government, a large army, or a stable life of any kind. He was on the run from an evil king. All he had was God—and it felt as though God were hiding his face. Some comfort!

David started his plea to God with these words: "Light up my eyes" (verse 3). When we go through a delay or depression, the light in our eyes dims. Our countenance becomes a kind of mask, a blank stare. Have you lost the light in your eyes during a delay? You're in good company. But David knew God can put that light back.

By the time David finished writing this psalm, it had become a song. He recalled the promise he had received when he was younger. He didn't understand the delay, but he knew God had promised him a dream and was a powerful promise keeper. David got the light in his eyes back. Was he delivered? Not yet. But he reconnected with the promise of his dream.

The Bible says that to end something is better than to begin it (see Ecclesiastes 7:8). God likes to hear our sighs, but he also loves turning them into songs while we wait for his timing to arrive.

THE WAITING GAME

In the book of Acts, the disciples' dreams seemed thwarted numerous times. Jesus wasn't the conquering king they thought he would be and didn't always meet their expectations. He died, then left them weak and powerless until the Holy Spirit came. Many times they saw their dreams apparently shattered, even by their own weaknesses and lack of faithfulness.

During the wait we are challenged by many distractions, pitfalls in the pathway, traps that test. If you know they are coming, they are easier to avoid. Here are three I have observed that try to derail people's dreams.

1. Cultural Distractions

Dream-centered living happens in spite of the culture around us rather than in agreement with it. The culture tells us it's all about the here and now; getting what we can; seeking pleasure, popularity, and profits. In the right balance, there's nothing wrong with those things, but when they are blown out of proportion, they become distractions that destroy dreams. Hunger for riches becomes blinding and corrupting. Excessive leisure and entertainment eat away your life. Popularity leads to incredible insecurity.

Every summer my family goes through the house and makes "to go" and "to stay" piles of our possessions. Recently I was surprised to find an iPod in my daughter's "to go" pile. It looked beat-up and may not have worked anymore, but I was surprised at how quickly things go from treasure to trash. Ten years earlier she had basically told us how awesome her life would become if only she had the new iPod. We got it for her, and there it was in a pile of junk she didn't want anymore.

In that same pile I saw a motorized scooter, a mermaid tail, and other toys my daughters had promised me would change their lives. A child's view is obviously less mature than an adult's, but how many times do we think the same thing—that a new phone or job or television series or vacation home will change our lives permanently for the better?

Dreamers stay focused on their dreams and don't set their hearts on temporary things that only become distractions.

2. Voices of Doubt

During the waiting you will get an earful from those dream busters, critics, and cynics we talked about. They can be friends, loved ones, or complete strangers. But usually the biggest dream buster is you! While waiting, it's easy to start discounting your dream, letting your logic take over. After all, dreams come with a lot of uncertainty. Noah must have had tons of questions when preparing the ark: What's a flood? What's rain? (It had never rained on the earth up to that point. God watered the earth from within, like dew on the ground.) How do I build a boat that big? How do I get the boat to the water? How am I going to round up all the animals?

What I love about Noah is that he didn't listen to those voices of doubt, even in his own head. He dared to be different, to go against the grain, to wait for the right time, and so he played a huge role in saving the world. Great people never follow the crowd or listen to dream busters. They decide deep in their spirits to go against the trend. Genesis 6:8 says, "Noah found favor in the eyes of the LORD." He made God smile. I want the same for you and me—to make God smile.

Voices of doubt, internal and external, didn't stop Noah from swinging a hammer. He kept moving in the direction of his dream, even during a very long wait. That takes remarkable confidence. Remember: the bigger the dream, the longer it usually takes.

3. Tempting Shortcuts

The longer a dream goes unfulfilled, the more tempting it is to take a shortcut. Most people will suggest you take a shortcut. It only makes sense to them. The way of the world is to make things happen on your own power. Society values speed.

At some point you'll be tested to think, *I know it's better to be patient and take time, but it seems if I take a shortcut things will go so much faster.* Beware of that temptation. Shortcuts are always shortsighted. They lengthen the delay and cause trouble down the road. You cannot seize control of your dream and make it go in a good direction.

Abraham took a shortcut to "help" God fulfill the dream of Abraham having a son. He slept with his maid to produce a son instead of waiting for God's promise. That wasn't God's idea. It caused a huge mess because Isaac and Ishmael, the two sons who spawned two nations, were always in conflict after that.

Jesus gives us a great example of patience. He waited until he was thirty years old to even begin his dream! Can you imagine? Most of his adult life was spent as an unknown carpenter in a small town. Yet he skipped the shortcuts and waited for the dream to come to full maturity.

Let's do the same: skip the shortcuts and spare ourselves problems.

6 months to God!

FOUR COMMITMENTS OF A DREAMER

What should we do during seasons of discipline and delay? Four simple things:

1. Wait for the Power

You are going to need the full power of your dream to work for you, not some watered-down, premature version. Jesus made his followers wait until they received power from on high. That's a promise for us, not just them. You will receive supernatural power for the task ahead if you don't rush ahead of God's timing.

I'm convinced that much of the dream-centered life is simply saying, *Okay, God. It doesn't make sense to me. All of culture is going the other direction. But I'm going to do exactly what you say.* That posture of patience and obedience is much more powerful than our own efforts.

2. Remember the Voice of God

Psalm 34:3 encourages us to "magnify the LORD." Does that mean make him bigger? No, but it means we make him bigger in our own lives. By doing this we make God's voice bigger than the voices of doubt in our own situation.

Imagine the dream busters who rose up against Noah and the pressure he got from his own family. I picture his three sons coming home from school saying, "Dad, why can't you have a normal job like everyone else? People are talking about the battleship in our front yard. It's social suicide."

The only way to endure voices of doubt for decades is to constantly remember the voice of God, to make it bigger and louder in your heart. As foolish as it may feel at times, reconnect with what he said about your dream. Do it in childlike confidence. Let God's voice be a shout and all else be a whisper.

3. Refuse to Believe What You See

This is especially personal for me. One of the great challenges in my life is to avoid the temptation of paying too much attention to what looks good and impressive on the outside and not enough attention to what is hidden on the inside. For example, as a pastor, I have a very public job each week to share a message from the platform. I want that message to change lives, to powerfully influence people in positive directions, to inspire and edify my listeners. But the truth is, I can see only a small percentage of the results my message produces in them. They may applaud or thank me afterward, but I cannot see what has happened on the inside. Maybe they will get in the car and forget everything I said by the time they get home.

Every week I force myself to refuse to believe only what I see, good or bad. If a message seems to bomb, I have to believe that God can make it powerful by using something I said in his own way. If a message gets a great response, I have to tell myself that outward displays of appreciation can be deceptive and addictive. I have to trust that by being faithful in study, preparation, and listening to God, the message will do its work out of sight. I may never see the results. But I press onward, believing in what I cannot see.

In the same way, your dream is developing even when you can't see it. It is maturing under the surface.

4. Lock In and Refuse to Quit

I am convinced that the middle of the dream determines whether or not we end successfully. How we behave in those delays determines our ultimate outcome. It's like those middle rounds of a boxing match that can seem tedious to the audience. That's where boxers score points or even land a surprise knockout. God works on us during the delay, and one thing he's putting into us is persistence, determination, endurance—spine.

Let me give you three *A*s that help me lock in to the dream-centered life even when it doesn't feel so dreamy.

Affiliation—There are actually times when a dream can seem embarrassing to us because it is delayed. It surely happened to Noah, Abraham, David, and every other Bible hero. One of the tests of waiting is whether or not we will continue to affiliate with our dream. Will we talk about it? Own it? Declare our belief in it? That can be hard to do when people are doubting, but taking a stand for a dream is more powerful when it seems unlikely than at any other time. Affiliate with your dream, even when it doesn't make you look good in the eyes of others.

Alignment—This means walking with someone in the same direction at the same pace. God's speed for fulfilling your dream is the right one. If you're falling behind or rushing ahead, it's not going to work. If you try to peel off and take a shortcut, that won't work either. Don't just affiliate with the dream; align yourself with God's timing and direction. Affiliation and alignment often don't make sense, but that's part of the journey.

Agreement—This simply means you are convinced that God's dream and his process are the best way for your life. Agreement with God is especially powerful in times of waiting and discouragement. It honors him when we affirm his path. Having watched so many dreams come to pass, I know what the end of the delay looks like. You will come to a place where you see that bend in the road as your best friend. You will thank yourself for affiliating, aligning, and agreeing with God during the disruptions, delays, and discipline.

The good news is the difficult season won't last forever. It may come to an end very suddenly, as I was just about to find out.

AN IDEA REBORN

My family and I were on vacation in New York City when I felt a strong but random impression in my soul: *Pray that you will meet with this specific pastor from Scottsdale.*

Yes, Lord. I will, I answered the Lord in my heart. Angel and my daughters and I were sitting in a restaurant in Manhattan. Ministry was the furthest thing from my mind. But the inner voice came again.

Pray that you will meet with this specific pastor from Scottsdale.

The impression wouldn't leave me alone, so I interrupted the conversation and said, "I know this sounds random, but I want you to pray with me. I feel like I have to talk to a certain pastor back home. There's something important there, and I don't know what. But I want to pray for an opportunity and favor to have that conversation."

My girls looked at me in a way that said, "You're kind of crazy. I thought we were on vacation. Are we going to pray all night?"

We bowed our heads, and I prayed that God would open a door for me to talk to this man and would show us his purpose and favor. We also prayed for him and his wife and their work in Scottsdale. I ended the prayer, and we went back to eating and talking as if nothing had happened.

The following week we were back in Phoenix. I typically study for my message at a coffee shop in town, but this week, for some reason, I went to a coffee shop I never go to. I was sitting there with my laptop open and my study materials around me when I felt a tap on my shoulder. I turned around. There was the man that God had told me to pray about seeing. We hadn't seen each other in fifteen years.

"Luke? What are you doing here?" he asked.

"That's a good question. I don't know," I said. "I don't usually come to this place, but I was on this side of town and wanted to study for my message. I have to tell you, my family was just praying for you and your wife. How are you doing?"

With that, this pastor sat down and began to pour out his heart about what had been happening at his church. They were in a season of real struggle. They had grown the church to a thousand members some time ago and bought property in north Scottsdale. Later, they built a new auditorium and campus on twenty-seven acres ten miles away. It was a beautiful campus with a thousand-seat auditorium and lots of classroom space. The pastor truly had a vision for excellence, and it showed in the architecture. But because of the change in location, many people left the church. The church went into decline, and then an economic recession hit. They had taken a $10 million loan for the property and were now upside down on it. After they filed Chapter 11 bankruptcy, the banks reorganized their debt and made the loan $3.1 million. The church had shrunk to a hundred people.

"Luke, it has been a real struggle for us over the past few years, and I feel like we need to find a young pastor to come in and lead the church," he said. "Would you help me find a pastor to take over?"

I felt a spark inside me and was bold enough to say, "I think I have the answer." I shared the vision of a multisite campus and the possibility of merging our churches. He nodded his head, and I could tell we were in unity about what to do. Right there we agreed to bring up the idea with our boards.

"By the way, is this your regular place?" I asked, gesturing to the coffee shop as we were parting ways.

"No, I rarely come to this coffee shop, and today I already had five cups of coffee," he said, laughing. "For some reason I just felt like getting another."

We both knew God had engineered the meeting.

Things sped ahead. Our boards met, prayed about merging the churches, and voted to do it. The Scottsdale church then brought it to a congregational vote, which passed nearly unanimously. Within four and a half months, we had our first multisite campus. I had barely lifted a finger to make it happen. Everyone knew it was God at work, not Luke Barnett or any other man.

There was one little thing I didn't know. The Scottsdale church had borrowed money from a local developer to build a nearly half-million-dollar lobby extension. This was in addition to the original bank loan. That handshake agreement still stood, meaning we now owed the developer $400,000. I had our architect call the developer right away to ask what our obligation was so we could honor the commitment.

On opening weekend, nine hundred people showed up to the Scottsdale campus. Among them was the developer we owed that money to. Within a week or so, he wrote me a letter saying he had rededicated his life to the Lord and wanted to make the Scottsdale campus his home church. He also said he would forgive the entire loan.

It was breathtaking to see God work so quickly to bring to life a dream that seemed dead. I was so grateful we hadn't made a stupid move and invested a ton of money in a property when God wanted to give us an existing twenty-seven-acre campus right across town. It would have taken us twenty years to build up a campus like this on our own strength. God had done it in eight weeks.

I know that during those years of waiting, some at our church wondered if I had given up on the multisite dream. I had quit talking about it. Maybe they thought I had gotten my signals crossed. Now it became clear to all of us that two years earlier we weren't ready for another campus from a leadership standpoint. Our ministries weren't as strong as they needed to be. We weren't developing great leaders to help staff other campuses. God knew that as badly as we wanted it, we weren't ready. Sometimes our dream can kill us if we get it too early. God delays so that our maturity matches our opportunity.

God had worked in me to humble me during that waiting time as well. Had all five aspects of the dream taken off simultaneously, my pride might have gone off the charts. I would have easily interpreted it as my own abilities bringing success. As ridiculous as it seems, that's how the human heart works. God made it happen in a way that left no room for me to claim victory in my own strength. I was so grateful for that.

A BIG HURDLE?

I knew that God might continue to move faster than we expected and that we needed to proceed with an idea that only made sense given our new multisite reality: a name change.

I told my dad, "We're going to have to do a name change." His response was immediate.

"Oh, Son, I don't know if you want to go there," he said. "People are really attached to our name. There's a big legacy worldwide."

"But we can't be Phoenix First Scottsdale or Phoenix First Tucson or whatever," I said. "It has to be more inclusive, bigger."

"I think it'll be a bigger mountain than you think," he warned.

I gave it a lot of thought, and in the end my dad's own example inspired me. The first thing he did when he came to pastor the church in Phoenix thirty-six years earlier was to change the name from First Assembly of God to Phoenix First Assembly because his vision was to go after the whole city. It hadn't hurt them then. Now our vision had grown beyond Phoenix to the whole state, and we needed a name that incorporated the whole network of churches we hoped to plant. We wanted to hold on to our legacy as a place of dreams while stepping into our destiny.

I was confident enough to bring it up with the church's board. To my surprise, and Dad's, they jumped on it right away and said, "Let's vote on it tonight."

I said, "Don't you guys feel bad about leaving our name behind?"

"No," they said. They were so excited about the way the multisite vision was unfolding that they wanted to act on it immediately.

We ran through a number of different possible names and came up with one we liked most: Dream City Church. The next Sunday I got up before the congregation and said, "Folks, the vision for this church is bigger than Phoenix now. Sometimes you have to leave behind what you have to get the new, bigger thing God is doing. We're going to have to do a name change. The board voted on it, and starting in thirty days at the launch of the new campus, we will no longer be Phoenix First but Dream City Church."

All the leaders held their breath to see what the people would do. They broke out clapping and cheering. You could feel the energy in the room. In a single moment we had overcome what threatened to be a major mountain to climb. People had seen the other four dreams coming together—the arts, the campus, small groups, and the conference—and our community was greatly encouraged by the clearly supernatural work being done in us and through us. Changing the name to include the new dream seemed natural.

Little did we know it would lead quickly to a third campus.

A few weeks after we opened the Scottsdale campus, my dad got a call from another pastor in town. This man had built a very large Lutheran church. In fact, this particular church was one of the most influential churches in America at one time. For a while it was drawing eleven thousand people each weekend, but the pastor had suffered health issues and the church had declined dramatically.

At lunch this man asked about Dream City Church.

"You went through a name change?" he asked my dad, knowing just how difficult a name change could be.

"Yes," Dad said.

"And now you have a church in Scottsdale?" the man asked. His eyes lit up as Dad told him about how it had miraculously unfolded.

"Do you think Luke would consider making us a Dream City church?" the man asked. Dad just about had a heart attack. The pastor shared what he felt God was speaking to him, about becoming stronger by merging with our church.

"Clearly, you guys have a big vision like I have," he said. "I mean, you even gave up your name to move into your new destiny. That's commitment."

God's wisdom became obvious to us. If we hadn't been willing to broaden our scope and make a potentially difficult change, this man might not have wanted to jump on board with us. Now the way was open. Within days I went to tour their campus of seventy-five acres, a two-thousand-seat auditorium, a gorgeous gym, sand volleyball courts, and a Christian school with eight hundred kids and a team that had just won the state football championship. I preached on Sunday to a crowd of about 450 people and was well received. Within a few short months, the church became our Dream City Church Glendale campus. On Easter Sunday 2016, we officially launched the church with nearly a thousand people attending. Immediately, attendance went up again, not because of my preaching, but because of God's blessing of the dream we were now sharing.

The multisite dream that had sat dormant for nearly three years came to life so quickly that I could hardly get my head around it sometimes. God had done more in a few months than I had seen in my entire ministry up to then. We now owned campuses that took fifty years for other men to build. Instead of slogging through the sometimes arduous process of planting new churches, God had handed us two incredible campuses in turnkey condition, with great assets, ministries, and people.

Remarkably, I never received a negative letter about the name change. There was just too much excitement about what God was doing. Ministry felt incredibly fun, inspired, and joyful. Yes, it was hard work. I was now preaching at two different campuses every Sunday morning and had hired campus pastors for those locations. I was overseeing a lot more. But in a way it felt effortless and so blessed. I am certain it was because we stayed in sync with God's dream and his timing.

We were wise to stay in agreement with him through the delays and let him unfold the dream when and how he wanted to.

Let's revisit the principles here:

- The bend in the road is not the end of the road. God slows us down for a number of reasons: to humble us, to build the character we need to accomplish the dream, to teach us endurance, and more. Delay is not denial. It's just delay, and it's often purposeful.

- While waiting, we have to guard ourselves against cultural distractions, voices of doubt, and tempting shortcuts. Each can threaten our dream. We must commit to wait for the right timing and shut out those voices of distraction, doubt, and temptation.

- When we endure through the waiting, God can work miraculously, as he did by accelerating our plans for a multisite campus. His timing is always so much better. In the end your dream will come to fruition more easily, you will be ready to handle it when it comes, and everyone will be in awe of how God did it.

9

Dreaming Well

I have learned more about the dream-centered life and leading people effectively than I ever knew was possible, and I still have a long way to go. Let me share several principles that I think are key to dreaming and leading well, as I have discovered in practice.

YOU DON'T NEED TO PUSH YOUR DREAM ON PEOPLE

Some people get hold of the dream for their life and then pursue a "fake it till you make it" strategy. They wear a "dream mask" of inauthenticity. They spend a lot of energy trying to convince people that their dream is happening.

I have never seen this approach work. It simply looks desperate. When people get caught up in making their dream appear to be working, they fall into a dangerous mind-set of valuing man's opinion over the truth. In the early church, a married couple named Ananias and Sapphira made that mistake, with disastrous results. They seemed to think they had to make everybody believe they were doing something significant, so they gave money publicly to the church out of a desire to be recognized. Then they lied, saying they gave the entire proceeds of a land sale, when in reality they gave only part (see Acts 5).

Maybe God did give Ananias and Sapphira a desire to give generously.

Maybe they weren't yet financially able to fulfill that dream but wanted to hurry into their dream. They confused the dream with their identity. They listened to a sweet-sounding lie that our dream gives us significance and standing in the world, that it determines our worth, that we can cut corners or be less than honest with people around us, that we don't have to fear God. In the end, the truth came out, and both Ananias and Sapphira died on the spot. It's a sobering story.

As awesome as your dream is, don't confuse it with your identity. Your dream will never cause you to be accepted, appreciated, and significant. You are all of those things already, just by being a child of God.

One of the best days of my life was when I got tired of being a phony. It's exhausting trying to present different images to different people. You have a hard time keeping your story straight, and in the end you're a basket case. You can't hide who you are from God anyway. Hebrews 4:13 has revolutionized my life. It says, "And no creature is hidden from his sight, but all are naked and exposed to the eyes of him to whom we must give account." Matthew 5:8 promises, "Blessed are the pure in heart, for they shall see God." And Psalm 139:23–24 reads,

> Search me, O God, and know my heart!
>   Try me and know my thoughts!
> And see if there be any grievous way in me,
>   and lead me in the way everlasting!

Those Bible passages have become my constant prayer—that God would relentlessly search me and that I would not let the dreams he gave me outgrow my fear of the Lord or my true identity.

If you want to see your dreams come to pass, be pure in heart. Don't confuse your identity with your dream. They are two totally separate things.

IT'S GOD'S DREAM, NOT YOURS

Our confidence must never be in our dream but in the Dream Giver, Jesus Christ. It may surprise you that the dream you are pursuing is ultimately not yours but his. His goal is not to bless your dream. Rather, he blesses his dream for your life. He made you for a purpose. That's what your dream is—God's purpose for you. Paul the apostle shared a profound truth when he wrote, "For we are his workmanship, created in Christ Jesus for good works, which God prepared beforehand, that we should walk in them" (Ephesians 2:10).

When did God put his dream in us? Yesterday? The day before? On the day of our birth? No, he had our dream prepared before the foundation of the world. That's hard to comprehend and is a great mystery we will understand only in eternity. But it's reassuring to know that when discovering your dream, you are looking not for something new but for something very old.

Hebrews 4:3 says that "his works were finished from the foundation of the world." Our dreams were actually finished before the world was even made. How is that possible? How can you finish something before you start? I'm not the deepest thinker, but I picture it like a new car on the showroom floor. Is the car really new? It actually started in the mind of the creator and was put on paper in the design room before being built in the factory. A new car is not really new. It has just become actual. In the same way, God had your dreams in mind long ago, and they are now becoming actual. "I know the plans I have for you," he told Jeremiah in the Bible, "plans for welfare and not for evil, to give you a future and a hope" (Jeremiah 29:11). Elsewhere he said, "Before I formed you in the womb I knew you" (1:5).

Your dream has been God's idea for a long time, so we worship not the dream but the one who gave it to us.

NOT EVERY DREAM IS YOURS

When I started in ministry, I battled with fitting in the mold. I tried to imitate all my heroes. When I tried to preach like Tommy Barnett, I preached on tiptoe the way he does. His calves are the size of bowling balls. All I got were cramps in my legs so they ached while I finished my messages.

I tried to share the gospel with people in person like David Wilkerson, who told gang members in New York, "You could cut me in a thousand pieces and lay them out in the street and every piece would love you."* I went to Los Angeles but didn't have the guts to tell any gang members that. I didn't seem to have Wilkerson's boldness.

I wanted to preach like the great English pastor Charles Spurgeon, who preached with a cigar in his hand. I thought of trying that, but it just wasn't me.

Every Christian biography I read made me act like a new hero. When I tried to emulate these heroes' call and their dreams, it fell flat. The reason is obvious to me now: God gave each of us different abilities and dreams. I'm not responsible for carrying out someone else's dream, and no one else is responsible for mine. God is never going to say, *Luke, why weren't you more like someone else?*

Don't sweat the dreams God didn't give you. In situations needing mercy, I still feel inadequate. I used to beat myself up for not measuring up in every category across the board. Then I gave up and focused on my areas of strength: leadership, evangelism, and teaching. I aim at developing those areas, not others. I am a much more effective dreamer

---

* David Wilkerson, John Sherrill, and Elizabeth Sherrill, *The Cross and the Switchblade* (New York: Berkley, 1962), 61.

and leader as a result of keeping my dream-centered life narrowly focused.

HEALTHY CULTURE IS HUGE

Some churches are known for their pressure-cooker environments. We've had staff members we hired from other places tell us they were glad to escape their former work environment. I believe strongly that the culture of your work, home, or school environment has to be cultivated all the time. It's like the air people breathe, and it affects everything.

In our environment, everything we do touches on the idea of dreaming, because that's who we are. It's in our DNA. We try to take time to celebrate wins and encourage each other. At other times we put our shoulders to the plow and push hard. We believe everyone we reach should develop as a dreamer. We expect our church services to be the most fun and inspiring hour and fifteen minutes of the week for people who attend. Because dreams are fun, inspiring, attractive.

Preparing a table for our guests is a big part of our church culture. Some churches see their meetings as family time, but that can lead to laziness or impropriety. When there are no guests at the dinner table, you interrupt each other and belch and get away with a lot of bad manners. But when guests are over, it's a whole different matter. We see our weekend church services as time for guests to join our family. Without getting uptight about it, we want to be on our best behavior. We create an environment of welcoming love. Our dream is to reach people with the message of Christ, so we prepare diligently for that dream.

That dynamic of preparing the table sets the tone for everybody. We usher and preach and sing and care for kids with excellence and a welcoming atmosphere in mind. People involved feel like they are on a mission. If a visitor comes one time, it may be our only opportunity to share the life-changing message of Jesus's love with that person. We are committed to doing our best.

When I was living in Southern California, I visited a massive Buddhist temple built on the side of a mountain in Hacienda Heights. I wanted to tour it and see what it was like. It turned into a very educational experience. When I walked up, someone met me and said, "You have to take your shoes off. You can't walk through the temple wearing shoes." That puzzled me, honestly, and produced questions in my mind: *Where will my shoes go? Will they be here when I get back? Why don't they allow shoes? What else don't they allow?*

As I walked around in my socks and looked at the inside of the temple, I wondered, *What kind of music am I hearing? Will there be a lesson I need to listen to? Where can I walk in the temple, and which places are out of bounds?* I was experiencing what many people experience when they go to church for the first time.

I keep that experience in mind every weekend, knowing that visiting a church can be intimidating and confusing. Visitors don't have to take their shoes off at Dream City Church, but I don't want anything else to get in their way of enjoying meeting with God and people.

Another big lesson I learned about having a healthy culture is that you don't have to fix every problem. When I first came on staff, I could see every problem right away. I wanted to fix them all. My dad said, "Slow down. If you give them time, many problems will solve themselves." I thought that was a Pollyannaish viewpoint, and I pushed back, saying, "There are issues here we have to deal with. That's leadership."

It took a while for me to see that Dad was right. It pays to be discerning about which problems to tackle. A lot of things do work themselves out. My natural reaction is still to attack problems and create solutions, but I have learned to be more patient and let time sort some things out. It often works out a lot better.

PRAY YOUR TRUE HEART

The greatest power any dreamer has is in prayer, which is why I come back to it. Prayer is by far the most important tool in my belt, and I can't remind you or myself enough to become a person of prayer on this journey of the dream-centered life.

I mentioned getting quiet and listening to God earlier. Now I'd like to encourage you to pray honest, even messy, prayers when needed.

Sometimes I realize I'm not talking to God about certain things because they don't seem spiritual enough. *What do people think about me? How is my job going? How am I going to get my message done for the weekend? How's my appearance?* When I go to pray, I put those thoughts aside and pray for a cure for cancer, remedies for world hunger, and solutions for other big problems. The words sound important, but it's not really what's in my heart.

True prayer is what you are actually thinking and feeling, not some prettified portrait. I've learned to give God the ugly version. He can handle it. We are his children, and children can be self-centered sometimes. It's no use trying to be so grown up that you hide who you really are.

One evening at dinner when we were kids, Dad walked in with bandages on his arm. Matthew, who was about ten, asked what the bandages were for.

"I visited the insurance man today and had some tests done so that when I die, you kids will get $300,000," Dad said.

The idea of our dad dying brought a sober mood to the table. Then Matthew piped up: "Apiece?"

Talk about a guileless heart! Simple, honest prayers work with God. He would rather hear our true inner reality than suffer through our facade.

Jeremiah the prophet is a hero of mine because he was a young man called to be a spokesman to the nations and he felt ill equipped. He didn't want to do it, but God promised him the words and protection he would need. Everywhere Jeremiah spoke God's words, he faced rejection and derision. The city leaders, the priests, and the common people all said, "Take a flying leap!" when they heard his words. They finally beat him and put him in stocks so people could laugh at him all day long.

Nice assignment, huh?

Jeremiah found refuge in pouring out his heart to God. It got messy sometimes. One time he basically told God, "You lied to me! And I allowed myself to be misled." It's one of the most remarkable prayers in the whole Bible.

> O LORD, you have deceived me,
>   and I was deceived;
> you are stronger than I,
>   and you have prevailed.
> I have become a laughingstock all the day;
>   everyone mocks me.
> For whenever I speak, I cry out,
>   I shout, "Violence and destruction!"
> For the word of the LORD has become for me
>   a reproach and derision all day long.
> If I say, "I will not mention him,
>   or speak any more in his name,"
> there is in my heart as it were a burning fire

shut up in my bones,
and I am weary with holding it in,
    and I cannot.
For I hear many whispering.
    Terror is on every side!
"Denounce him! Let us denounce him!"
    say all my close friends,
    watching for my fall.
"Perhaps he will be deceived;
    then we can overcome him
    and take our revenge on him." . . .

Cursed be the day
    on which I was born!
The day when my mother bore me,
    let it not be blessed!
Cursed be the man who brought the news to my father,
"A son is born to you,"
    making him very glad.
Let that man be like the cities
    that the LORD overthrew without pity;
let him hear a cry in the morning
    and an alarm at noon,
because he did not kill me in the womb;
    so my mother would have been my grave,
    and her womb forever great.
Why did I come out from the womb
    to see toil and sorrow,
    and spend my days in shame? (Jeremiah 20:7–10, 14–18)

What a messy prayer! You've got to really hate life when you curse the man who passed out cigars when you were born—to wish that your mother's womb had been your grave. And yet those pain-filled words become the passwords to a place of refuge in God. In the same chapter Jeremiah said,

> But the LORD is with me as a dread warrior;
>> therefore my persecutors will stumble;
>> they will not overcome me.
> They will be greatly shamed,
>> for they will not succeed.
> Their eternal dishonor
>> will never be forgotten.
> O LORD of hosts, who tests the righteous,
>> who sees the heart and the mind,
> let me see your vengeance upon them,
>> for to you have I committed my cause.
>
> Sing to the LORD;
>> praise the LORD!
> For he has delivered the life of the needy
>> from the hand of evildoers. (verses 11–13)

Nothing had really changed. Jeremiah had to go out the next day to speak the same words to the same resistant crowd. But he found a place of refuge that comes only from getting really honest with God.

Adversity is part of your dream. Bank on it. But we have a refuge that gives us protection and strength. We can speak like Jeremiah did, pouring out our hearts. Don't worry about getting it wrong. Lay it all out.

Echo King David's unvarnished, uncensored prayers in Psalms. Pray the real you.

You're going to need those messy prayers. Your dream will tempt you to worry and be anxious until you learn to successfully resist. In Philippians 4:6 Paul encouraged us, "Do not be anxious about anything, but in everything by prayer and supplication with thanksgiving let your requests be made known to God." He linked anxiety and prayer, making anxiety our reminder to pray. In that way, worry can be a useful tool if it drives us to our knees.

Each morning I arrive on campus early because I'm an early riser. I sit in my car for a few moments or take a walk around the campus and pour my heart out to God. I'm glad people can't hear some of the prayers I pray because I would probably get fired. They're messy, just like Jeremiah's words. Almost every day there's a challenge I'm facing that requires me to bare my heart to God. *I'm not the husband I need to be. Help me. I have to make a decision that will affect this church going forward. Help me. I'm really upset with this person or situation. Help!*

I always find the power and strength to walk into the office and do what he has called me to do. Messy, humble prayers draw God's grace like nothing else I know.

NEXT-LEVEL DREAMING

There will be times when God wants to take our dreams to a higher level of faith and blessing than ever. At those times, he often tests us in a stronger way, the way he tested Abraham by telling him to sacrifice Isaac, the son of the promise. Let me offer a few observations about these key seasons and what they might look like in your life.

Next-Level Dreaming Always Involves Sacrifice

"No pain, no gain," people say. No guts, no glory. God always tests us in something we love. He is not content to take a back seat to anything else we have. He wants to know, *What do you love the most, me or the dream I gave you?* The sacrifice he demands can be huge.

Jesus put it like this in Matthew 10:37: "Whoever loves father or mother more than me is not worthy of me, and whoever loves son or daughter more than me is not worthy of me."

That's pretty intense. If God is asking you for something that close to your heart, it's because he is getting ready to move you to a brand-new level in your dream.

The Sacrifice Will Not Line Up with Human Understanding

"Take your son, your only son Isaac, whom you love, and go to the land of Moriah, and offer him there as a burnt offering on one of the mountains of which I shall tell you" (Genesis 22:2). God's command must have perplexed Abraham. God had promised that Isaac would become a great nation. How could he be the father of a great nation if he were dead?

Human logic can get in the way when the sacrifice doesn't make sense. *God, why would you give me this house when they are foreclosing on me? Why would you give me this job when they're downsizing me? Why would you give me this child who's causing me such heartache?*

It's a test. Will you be faithful even when you don't understand? When logic has left the building?

The next verse is one of my favorites in the Bible: "So Abraham rose early in the morning" (verse 3). If there were ever a day to sleep in or dawdle at the coffee shop, this was it. But Abraham was quick to respond to God. He didn't understand the why, but he didn't argue. He saddled his donkey before the sun rose, took two men and Isaac, split some wood, and went on the fearsome journey. I love that.

There are some situations where you won't find answers in friendly counsel, your spouse, your parents, books, conferences, education, logic, hard thinking, or anything else. Some situations just make no sense, and nobody can help. You just have to obey.

Next-Level Dreaming Requires Faith That Goes All the Way

As Abraham grabbed the knife to kill Isaac, he may have thought, *Okay, God, I did what you asked. I got up early. I climbed the mountain. I brought the boy. Now you can stop me.* But heaven was silent. The command was not to get up early or climb the mountain or simply bring Isaac. The command was to sacrifice him. And now Abraham came to the point of decision.

If you're still waiting for God to come through, then you haven't completed the test yet. The test isn't that you are sincere or willing. The test is that you go all the way.

Why does God take us through tests when he knows the outcome in advance? Two reasons that I can see:

1. God wants to shows us where we stand. We gain humility and confidence in God through the experience. Abraham wouldn't have known how committed he was to obeying God if he hadn't gone all the way to obey.

2. God desires experiences with us. He knows all things factually and is present everywhere. But he chooses not to know everything experientially. That's why he came to earth as a man—to experience humanity. He wants more than factual knowledge. He wants to feel our love and loyalty

and passion for him. That's why the Bible says God inhabits the praises of his people (see Psalm 22:3, ASV). Does he need those praises? Absolutely not. He was doing fine a billion years before we got here. But he enjoys the praises of his people. He loves the experience of being first in our lives. So he creates scenarios where it's hard for us to put him first. He enjoys the feeling when we do, and he shares that feeling with us. That's why he told Abraham, "Now I know that you fear God, seeing you have not withheld your son, your only son, from me" (Genesis 22:12). God knew it experientially and emotionally now, not just factually.

That's why it's important to fall in love with Jesus. He knows every fact about you, but he can't enjoy you experientially unless you let him. He's after far more than factual data. He is a God of love and passion. He wants your heart.

The Reward Will Be Far Greater Than the Sacrifice

It's hard to see the reward during the test. Because Abraham had the guts to go through with it until the Lord said "Stop!" he did indeed become the father of a great nation and a blessing to the entire earth. The reward was billions of times bigger than the sacrifice he was about to make. But I'm sure he didn't grasp that reality when raising the knife over his dream.

Each of us will come to places where God wants to elevate us to the next level of our dream, and it usually involves these kinds of difficult sacrifices. It's when we have to believe more than ever that God is just and fair, kind and loving, and that he always gives back far more than we are willing to sacrifice.

SERVE THE POOR

One night before we were married, Angel and I went to the movies. At this particular theater they hire ticket takers who are special-needs persons, whom I love. On this night we noticed that one of the ticket takers was in the parking lot on a break and two older teenagers had stolen his bow tie. They were playing keep-away with it. It was so cruel. I turned to Angel to say, "Can you believe this?" But she wasn't there. I caught sight of her striding through traffic to where the boys were. She stuck her finger in their faces and said, "Give it back right now!" She grabbed that bow tie and handed it back to the worker. Right then I thought, *I'm going to marry that girl.*

I thank God I have a wife, mother and father, sister and brother, and church who fight for the underdog. Their attention always goes to the poor and least in society. If you want to add rocket fuel to your dream, make sure it serves the poor somehow. Give away a percentage of your profits. Spend time volunteering to serve. Build it into your dream. God will bless it even more.

Every Saturday night, members of our church go to strip bars in a certain area of town to minister to girls stuck in prostitution. They give each of them a rose and say, "You matter. Here's a card. If you ever need help, call us." They pray and talk with the girls as much as they can. I'm convinced that kind of ministry is a major reason God is expanding our vision to include the whole state of Arizona.

We also were moved by the plight of kids who age out of the foster-care system in our state. There are nineteen thousand kids in foster care in Arizona. When they reach age eighteen, they get a plastic garbage bag to put their possessions in and are turned out onto the streets. They usually have nowhere to go.

We stepped in and said, "If foster-care homes call us when kids age out, we will come with a suitcase full of supplies and invite those young people to live at our Dream Center for a while, to get their bearings."

The first time I shared that vision with the staff, our brilliant drama director, Mark Stoddard, came to me and said, "You're not going to believe this, but I have written a one-hour one-act play to create awareness of the foster-care plight. If you're open to it, I'd like to cooperate with the foster-care ministries in town to host a night here at the church to launch this ministry."

We did just that, filling the building with two thousand people, launching our foster-care ministry and receiving two hundred donated suitcases, each packed with everything a kid aging out would need to survive for a week. Now at the Phoenix Dream Center, we have a whole floor for young people from foster care. We also have rooms set aside for veterans who need a place to get their lives back together. A vocational center helps them learn a new trade.

When you make the poor and needy part of the DNA of your dream, God will always, always bless you beyond what you expect.

Let's encapsulate the lessons from this chapter:

- Don't fake it till you make it. Everybody recognizes a bluffer. If you need to push your dream on people to make it happen, then you're not working in God's timing and strength. Ditch the image-building campaign. Authenticity is much more attractive—and effective.

- Remember, it's ultimately God's dream, not yours. He is responsible for bringing it to pass. We are his junior partners.

- Some dreams aren't yours. They belong to other people. You can encourage them, even support them financially, but none of us have time to personally participate in every dream.
- It all comes back to prayer. When we tell God what we're actually thinking and feeling, it is a life-giving dialogue. Practice simple, honest prayers. They'll get you much further than attempts to sound spiritual.
- Next-level dreaming is when God calls us to a higher level of sacrifice and commitment. It often doesn't make sense and requires more faith than we think we have. But the reward is always much greater than the sacrifice.
- Make serving the poor a regular part of your life. No matter what your dream is, serving the poor is central to the dream-centered life.

10

Characteristics of a Dreamer

I was attending a political breakfast recently to pray the closing prayer. After the event, a United States senator ran up to me and grabbed my hand.

"Luke, how's your dad?" he said. "He's like a father of this city. I admire and respect him so much. Please tell him how much I love him."

That kind of thing happens all the time because of how many years my dad sowed in Phoenix. I was at a conference at Saddleback Church when Rick Warren walked by our table. He asked where we were from, and when I said, "Phoenix, Arizona," he looked at me and said, "Pastor Tommy Barnett. That man loves Jesus so much. I have followed your dad's work all the way back when he was in Iowa."

A lot of people think that dreamers are flakes, shallow people with slim character. I don't find that to be true at all. Great dreamers are by nature men and women of great character. They have to be to stand the test of time. Reputation is what others say about you, but character is who you are when you're by yourself. It's the real you.

There are six qualities I see in every dreamer, and we would all do well to make them our life's pursuit. These characteristics should get more noticeable in your life as your dream grows. If not, there's a real problem. Here we go.

INTEGRITY

Integrity is basic to the dream-centered life. Without it, there is no real success. Our world is in a real integrity crisis. Military leaders and politicians share secrets for money. CEOs serve prison terms for fraud and price fixing. Ministries fall to scandals. Proverbs 10:9 says, "Whoever walks in integrity walks securely, but he who makes his ways crooked will be found out." We watch that happen right before our eyes.

One time a couple asked my dad to perform their wedding ceremony. He agreed, then got a call from Brian Houston of Hillsong Church in Sydney, Australia.

"Tommy, I'd like you to come preach at our world conference," Brian said. Dad accepted and considered the invitation one of the greatest honors of his life. Then he checked his schedule—the wedding was on that very date. The couple surely would have understood if Dad had bowed out, but he is a man of his word. He called Brian and said, "I can't go. I committed to perform a wedding at my church." So Dad missed the Hillsong conference.

To add to the cringe factor, that couple's marriage lasted less than two years. Their vows didn't stay intact, but my dad's integrity did. He didn't take the easy way out. He kept his word.

Integrity is developed in small, daily decisions you probably don't even remember making. They are the building blocks of any successful dream. David built integrity tending his flocks alone. Saul of Tarsus, who later became known as Paul, learned integrity for three years in the Arabian Desert, out of everyone's sight. Jesus learned it for thirty years before his public ministry. Moses learned it for forty years in the desert.

I talked about Joe Martinez's journey in Southern California with me, and then at Dream City Church. When he took his most recent post with us, big things began happening under his leadership. Mom's Pantry took off, our worship arts headed in exciting new directions, and more. People might have thought Joe had the Midas touch, but they didn't see the decade Joe spent at lower levels of authority. I remember him being on nursery duty, cleaning up trash, doing whatever needed to be done. Integrity is built in slow motion, through small, daily decisions.

Are you paying attention to those unseen decisions and attitudes that can develop integrity in you?

Mike Singletary, a former NFL player, once said his team spent eighty hours a week for nine minutes of glory in a game. If you count the actual time spent playing football in a game, it amounts to just nine minutes. The rest of the time the clock is ticking down. But those eighty hours a week were spent watching film of opponents, doing drills on the practice field, eating just the right things, pumping weights, getting rest. The players wanted to be their best when it counted. They were building strength and integrity off the field and out of sight for just a few moments of glory in the spotlight.

That's how integrity is built. One day at a time, one courageous, small decision at a time. Saying no to temptation. Forgiving someone rather than holding a grudge. Giving rather than getting. Serving rather than being served. These actions build strength into your dream.

I think of Todd Beamer, one of the heroes of United Airlines Flight 93 that went down on 9/11. His wife, Lisa, wrote about the decisions Todd had made before that day. As he was working toward his MBA, he wrote in his journal his life goals:

- "Be a strong Christian, know direction, and be disciplined.
- Be a father with integrity.
- Be able to build friendships, take care of and assist friends.
- Love my wife and support her efforts. . . .

- Strive to be like my father—to be respected even when I'm not around. . . .
- Be compassionate to others."*

Todd and Lisa led a small group for couples at their church. He served in children's ministry. He was like any of us—ordinary. But he chose integrity, and it prepared him for the great moment of crisis in his life.

Maybe you're like me. Sometimes I think I've got a lot of ground to make up to be a Todd Beamer.

One morning I was driving out of our neighborhood when the steering wheel hit my cup of coffee and it spilled all over my lap. My legs were burning and the front of my pants was soaked. I kept driving and reached for a towel. Then I looked up, and I was on the wrong side of the road with oncoming traffic just forty feet away. I swerved quickly back into my lane. Everyone around me got upset. A guy going my same direction held up the half peace sign. Expletives were flying out of his mouth. I got so angry at this guy for freaking out. *Where's the compassion?* I thought. *Does he think I went into the opposite lane on purpose?*

So I did what every good spiritual leader does. I got in front of him and slammed on my brakes. He slammed on his brakes to avoid hitting me. Now we were both boiling mad. I pulled over and put my car in reverse. Believe it or not, we were about to have a confrontation on the side of the road.

Then it was as if I heard the clear voice of God in my heart: *Own it, Luke. Apologize.*

I knew more was at stake than a nasty exchange. My heart was on the line. Our cars drew even, and I rolled my window down.

"Dude, I am so sorry," I said. "I spilled coffee all over my lap and was trying to wipe it off. Please forgive me. That was an accident."

---

* Lisa Beamer and Ken Abraham, *Let's Roll!* (Carol Stream, IL: Tyndale, 2002), 100–101.

His face turned from Tasmanian devil to benign little bunny.

"Oh, man. I'm sorry I reacted that way," he said. "I get it. No problem."

We went from being rage-filled enemies to being chummy for those few seconds.

"God bless you, man. Have a great day," I said. We waved and went on with our days.

I drove away from that moment thinking, *I don't always win those internal battles, but this time I chose integrity. I wish I always did! But I'm getting better.*

HUMILITY

Humans are the only species whose reaction to a pat on the back is a head that swells up.

The Bible is clear that the most dangerous place to occupy on earth is the place of pride. The safest place is in the habit of humility. Humility is like oil in the engine of the dream-centered life. Without it, nothing works. Proverbs 29:23 tells us that pride will bring us low, but the lowly in spirit will obtain honor. The Bible says that God saves humble people but actively brings down proud people (see 2 Samuel 22:28). Jesus promised, "Whoever exalts himself will be humbled, and whoever humbles himself will be exalted" (Matthew 23:12). Proverbs 11:2 says, "When pride comes, then comes disgrace, but with the humble is wisdom." The book of James warns that "God opposes the proud but gives grace to the humble" (4:6).

Convinced yet?

Every time you get a compliment, it's a test. Will you get egotistical about it? Or will you give that compliment right to God? He tests our humility with praise (see Proverbs 27:21). He is seeing what our character is made of.

God also uses our mistakes to test our humility. If you can be open about your mistakes, laugh at yourself, and use your foibles to help others, it's a good sign. Humor and humility come from the same word. Humble people can laugh at themselves. Proud people can't stand to. As they say, if you learn to laugh at yourself, you'll have plenty of material for the rest of your life.

My dad made an embarrassing verbal gaffe one Father's Day. He used to hand out socks to dads on that day. He had an extra pair and decided to award them to the father in attendance who had the most children. From the platform he asked guys to raise their hands if they had five, six, seven children, and so on. He finally identified a guy who had nineteen daughters! He brought him up on the stage and said, "Tell us again how many children you have."

"I have nineteen daughters," the man said.

People applauded, and before I tell you what Dad said next, let me give a quick sidebar. Dad used to preach on Solomon having more than seven hundred wives. One of his jokes was, "That's a lot of pantyhose hanging on the shower bar."

Now he tried to use that line, but he garbled it. What came out of his mouth was this: "Nineteen daughters. Wow! That's a lot of hose in the bathroom." Say that out loud, and you'll see why everybody in the place was cringing and groaning. Dad had no idea what he'd said.

Now Dad tells that story at pastors' conferences to encourage other guys. People are always more encouraged by a leader's mistakes than his victories.

Mistakes are perhaps the best tool for keeping us humble. Embrace them. Paul said he learned to glory in his weaknesses rather than his strengths (see 2 Corinthians 12:9). That's a profound truth of a dream-centered life. So many today work hard to keep their image up. People hire image consultants to tell them how to walk right, talk right, eat right, dress right, and project success. The pervasiveness of social media encourages daily image building, as if we were all celebrities.

Image is the enemy of humility. The Bible says to clothe yourself with humility (see Colossians 3:12). Humility never goes out of style. It's how to dress for success. People want to be around humble people. There's something real and approachable about them.

Here are four memorable ways to think about it:

1. Stay humble or you will stumble.
2. Remember the lesson of the whale: "When you get to the top and you're ready to blow, that's when they harpoon you every time. So stay low."
3. Treat praise like bubblegum—you can chew on it for a while, but don't swallow it.
4. Image vanishes in a puff. Character lasts forever.

DEPENDABILITY

As an athlete at the small high school I attended, I traveled all over the state. We played all the old mining towns and drove hundreds of miles to get to our games. Yet at every game, there were my parents. I could see them from the field or the basketball court, and it meant so much to me that they were there. They kept their word that they would be at my games, and it made a huge impression on me as a young man.

Everyone admires people who can be counted on. Simply living up to our words is a basic element of character.

LIVING BY PRIORITIES

I shared earlier about using our schedules as powerful tools for our dreams. The average person lives around twenty-eight thousand days, give or take a few. Let's be purposeful about how we spend each one. Don't fritter away time on nonessentials. Think through how you spend your time. Jettison the distractions and make room for your dream.

GENEROSITY

We all will be remembered for what we gave, not what we received.

I remember being eleven years old at the first building our church occupied in Phoenix. The church had just sold that campus and had money to buy property but not enough to build a building. Dad called on people to sacrifice and bring possessions to give toward building the new church facility.

At an evening service, people came forward and put their pledges into a chest. Some even put valuables and money there. It was clear that many were sacrificing for this new vision.

Dad called a time-out right in the middle of the service and summoned his family to the platform for a private meeting. He was crying.

"I feel led to do something I told my dad I would never do," he said to us. He explained that when he was fifteen he earned $5,000 and put it into a mutual fund. His dad made him promise never to touch it until he retired. Pastors can opt out of paying Social Security, and Dad had done so earlier in life. He would need the money in that mutual fund later. Over time that $5,000 grew to $235,000.

"Kids, this could be your inheritance, which is why I won't do this without your agreement," he said, "but I just feel so strongly that I need to give it all to the church."

I was so young I didn't really know the value of money, so I said, "Yeah, give it away." Mom and Kristie and Matthew agreed too. Dad put a pledge into that chest, committing all of it to the new church building. He wasn't the only one digging deep. Many people lived on less so they could sow into the new campus and the dream of reaching the entire city. Some lived in smaller homes so the church could fulfill its God-given dream.

If those people had not given, we wouldn't be talking about it now, and the church would have remained in that small building. It would not have reached the city. It would not have lived the dream.

Our legacy is never in what we keep but in what we give away. God plays a game with us called "Who Can Give More?" You'll never win. I've been playing this game for twenty years. The more I give to his purposes, the more he gives to me. It's his way of making us like him: generous.

SPIRITUALITY

When we sincerely live by God's values, we receive favor with God and people (see Proverbs 3:3–4). People are naturally drawn to those who genuinely love God without being sentimental or syrupy. They feel the purity in it, and it brings a feeling of safety, stability, and depth to the relationship.

By contrast, wicked people are forgotten. That was very much on my mind one time when I was playing a pickup game of basketball at a local park. The game was getting intense, and right in the middle of it, this kid took a cheap shot at me. He needlessly elbowed me in the stomach while running down the court. I was offended. I thought, *I'm going to log that, and if I get the opportunity, I'll get him back.* Sure enough, I saw an opportunity and returned the cheap shot to the guy.

Two days later I was reading 1 Peter 3:9, which encourages us not to return evil for evil but to give blessings for evil. I prayed, *God, if there's something you want to tell me about this passage, please do.* He brought that incident to mind, and I could see how ugly my actions and attitude had been. I knew I had to make it right. I didn't have the guy's number so I called the guys I knew who had been in that game, and they gave me his contact information. I was the senior pastor of a prominent church in town, and here I was calling a teenage kid to apologize to him.

I finally got in touch with him and said, "I'm very sorry. I shouldn't have responded that way."

He was surprised I had called, but we both knew I had done the right thing.

If it's possible for me to learn a lesson like this, it's possible for everyone. Every time we choose character over self-gratification, we win, even if we look weak in the sight of people. It delights the heart of God. It is a resounding choice to follow the dream no matter what it costs or what we look like.

Let's look at these characteristics one more time:

- Integrity. Nothing of value gets built without it. It is at the foundation of your dream.
- Humility. Stay humble or you will stumble.
- Dependability. Build a track record of being reliable and standing by your word.
- Living by priorities. Use each of your twenty-eight thousand days purposefully and without regrets.
- Generosity. It not only shapes our hearts but also builds our legacies. People are remembered not by what they earned or received but by what they gave.
- Spirituality. We need to put God's interests over our own in every situation—even in traffic or at a pickup basketball game.

11

Dreaming with Confidence

Having seen some of my dreams come to pass, I have a much different perspective on my early battles in Ohio and Southern California. I'm grateful for them. I wouldn't change a thing.

They were preparing me for the bigger dream God had in store that I couldn't see yet. Things now come across my desk every week that could knock the wind out of a young leader, but I'm seasoned enough that they don't faze me. God built strength into my ministry through suffering. Psalm 119:71 says, "It is good for me that I was afflicted, that I might learn your statutes."

When I was younger, I was leading without a dream. I was living without a dream. I relied on my organizational skills, my teaching ability, my own leadership tools. To be honest, it was an inferior way of leading and an inferior way of living. What makes me sad is that the vast majority of churches and organizations, as well as people and families, seem to be chugging along without a God-sized dream to propel them. They deal with regular burnout. Things seem perpetually mundane. They stop expecting great things from themselves or God. It seems to take monumental effort to get by and make it one more day.

I've been there. I lived and led from a secondhand revelation. I've had the long nights questioning why life seems so dull and difficult. I've gritted my teeth and moved ahead without a white-hot vision drawing me into the future.

The dream-centered life is so much more fulfilling and gratifying. There's really no comparison, no feeling in the world that touches it. When you get a dream, you don't want to quit because it's so exciting. You finally feel you are tapping your full potential. You feel fully alive.

Before becoming a dreamer, I put my focus on methods and man-made efforts. These days I count on God to make me his mouthpiece. I spend more time in preparation, getting my heart and mind right before I get up to teach. My goal is not just to give sound advice but, as best I can, to proclaim God's message for the people. Sunday morning could be the most critical forty minutes of their week. I have a lot more respect now for what I say in that window of time. Before discovering my dream, I was a communicator. Now I feel I have an authoritative word to say. It comes back to the dream. It gives me great purpose and confidence when I stand up there. I know that God painted a picture in my mind. I'm leading us toward something beyond what we might have cooked up.

My confidence is no longer in myself.

When you become a dream-centered person, people place more confidence in you. They know they are no longer following a man's ideas or creativity. Your vision is inspired, and it's obviously not tied to your personality or talent or good looks. Everyone knows my limitations as a pastor. They know I don't have the highest IQ in the world. But they know I'm a dreamer, and together we see that there are no limits to where that dream will take us. My leadership is now grounded in something beyond myself.

We see this shift in the Bible. In Acts 1 the disciples felt they needed to replace Judas, who had betrayed Jesus and killed himself. Two qualified candidates stood out to them, and they were torn over which one to choose. Guess what these fathers of the faith did to fill the spot? They cast lots. Imagine. It's like they were in Vegas tossing the dice and saying, "Come to papa. Come on, lucky number. Show us what to do." The lot fell to Matthias, who became the twelfth disciple.

That decision seems to have been made in an inferior way. But in a way, they had no choice. The Holy Spirit had not yet come and was not available to guide them. They hadn't experienced heaven's supernatural energy and direction. In the very next chapter, Acts 2, the Holy Spirit did come in a powerful way. After that you never see them cast lots again. Their decisions were made with the counsel of the Holy Spirit, who gave them direction. Life wasn't chance anymore.

For many people, life is mostly chance. They make decisions according to their own intelligence or even by randomly choosing. They remind me of the big, burly lumberjack who walked into a hardware store and was approached by a salesman.

"We've got a new machine that cuts down trees twenty times faster than an ax," the salesman boasted. "It's called a chain saw."

"Twenty times faster? Give me one of those things!" the lumberjack said. He promptly paid for his new tool and walked out. Two days later, he burst back into the store.

"This thing didn't help me at all," he said. "I worked all day long and not one tree came down."

"Let's take a look," the salesman said and took the chain saw into his hands. He yanked the cord and started it up.

The lumberjack jumped back and said, "What's that noise?"

The power is in the dream. It's time to turn it on.

STILL OVERCOMING CHALLENGES

Let me assure you that we continue to face challenges. Going to four campuses was hugely challenging. Just as we were adding the Scottsdale campus, we temporarily lost our new campus pastor. He and his son were riding dirt bikes when a deer jumped out in front of him. He hit the deer, flew off the bike, and broke seven ribs and his collarbone.

On our first Sunday as a multisite church, we hoped to link both campuses with a live video feed, but it wouldn't work. The technology at one church location wasn't talking to the technology at the other. Our team was working very late on Saturday night to make all the new technology work for our services the following morning. As our media director was drilling holes in a thick metal plate that would be used for a monitor stand, suddenly the high-powered drill spun the plate, which caught his thumb, cutting part of it off and hitting an artery. He had to have surgery that very night.

It wasn't like the dream arrived on our doorstep and we have lived in placid perfection ever since. At times my anxiety and frustration went through the roof as we faced setbacks, but this just reminded me where my confidence was. When you have a dream, you snap back more quickly. You don't have to search for a new answer to every problem because you know everything relates back to your dream.

Ancient Israel was commanded by God to conquer seven nations that occupied their Promised Land. Each nation was larger and stronger than Israel. When Joshua led Israel across the Jordan River, it was considered an act of war. That's why God said three times, "Be strong and courageous" (Deuteronomy 31:6–7; Joshua 1:9).

Joshua spent the rest of his life in battle, but each battle brought the blessing of taking new territory. He lived and fought for the dream. When God commands us to fulfill our destiny, it always comes with the promise that he will fight with us.

If you are in a battle, let me encourage you that there's a purpose for it. Battles qualify us for God's blessing. He trains us through battles to handle bigger dreams.

A Pipeline of Leadership

Recently I got a call from Dr. Kent Ingle, president of Southeastern University in Florida. He and his team asked if we would be interested in starting an extension of their campus on our campus. We decided to do this and entered a partnership called Dream City University, powered by Southeastern University. It combines what we do best and what Southeastern does best. Students get a great education and are part of our culture for four years, doing hands-on ministry while they learn. We're excited about having tracks for the arts, building Dream Centers in urban areas, youth ministry, worship music, children's ministry, and more. Some of those graduates will help us plant more Dream City Churches.

That partnership has changed the way our staff members see their jobs. Now we're not only providing ministry in a church context but also training young people in a university-like atmosphere on campus. Our staff members are now teachers, taking kids through some of these tracks. It's about equipping and raising up leaders, which is a whole new paradigm for us.

I still remember the first time I talked about Arizona being known as a Christian state. My staff chuckled. Some thought I had overreached. But that dream was from God, and the elements are coming into place. We haven't completely figured out yet how to become a multisite church with campuses in many other cities. But it looks a lot more possible than it ever did before. I would love to plant one church a year for the next twenty years, putting a Dream City Church in every city of significance in Arizona. We are even thinking beyond multisites to microsites. If there's a family who lives an hour away and wants to be part of us, the technology is available for them to live-stream the broadcast, invite friends and neighbors, and have church in their home. We could have many microsites with no campus at all. Already, people have asked if we would support that kind of ministry.

As you see our dream moving ahead, I hope you are encouraged to do whatever it takes to pursue your dream-centered life. Each of us has a few short years. I think about the richest places in the world—cemeteries. It's not because people are buried with their valuables but because they die with their dreams unfulfilled. There are songs not composed, books not written, cures not developed for fear of failure. So many dreams are taken to the grave unrealized. If you could mine the dreams from one cemetery and bring them to fruition, you'd be the wealthiest person alive.

Let's use our time for more than dreamless living. Let's not make the graveyards any richer. Let's give everything we have to live the high calling of the dream-centered life.